Making Every Day Count

Daily Readings for Young People on
Solving Problems, Setting Goals,
& Feeling Good About Yourself

Pamela Espeland and Elizabeth Verdick

free spirit
PUBLiSHiNG®

Helping kids
help themselves™
since 1983

Library of Congress Cataloging-in-Publication Data
Espeland, Pamela
     Making every day count : daily readings for young people on solving problems, setting goals & feeling good about yourself / Pamela Espeland and Elizabeth Verdick
          p.   cm.
     Includes indexes.
     Summary: Presents 366 quotations, advice, and affirmations to help readers face challenges, plan for the future, and appreciate their unique and wonderful qualities.
     ISBN 1-57542-047-3
     1. Goal (Psychology)—Quotations, maxims, etc.—Juvenile literature.
     2. Problem Solving—Quotations, maxims, etc.—Juvenile literature.
     3. Self-esteem—Quotations, maxims, etc.—Juvenile literature. 4. Success—Psychological aspects—Quotations, maxims, etc.—Juvenile literature.
     [1. Goal (Psychology) 2. Self-esteem. 3. Success.] I. Verdick, Elizabeth. II. Title.
     BF505.G6.E76   1998
     158.1—dc21   98-42502
                                                                                           CIP
                                                                                            AC

Cover and book design by Marieka Heinlen

15 14 13 12 11 10 9 8
Printed in the United States of America

Free Spirit Publishing Inc.
217 Fifth Avenue North, Suite 200
Minneapolis, MN 55401-1299
(612) 338-2068
help4kids@freespirit.com
www.freespirit.com

Free Spirit Publishing is a member of the Green Press Initiative, and we're committed to printing our books on recycled paper containing a minimum of 30% post-consumer waste (PCW). For every ton of books printed on 30% PCW recycled paper, we save 5.1 trees, 2,100 gallons of water, 114 gallons of oil, 18 pounds of air pollution, 1,230 kilowatt hours of energy, and .9 cubic yards of landfill space. At Free Spirit it's our goal to nurture not only young people, but nature too!

g green press INITIATIVE

To John and Jonah
PLE

To Dan and Olivia
EV

Contents

Introduction

If you want to improve your problem-solving skills, boost your ability to set and reach goals, and feel good about yourself every day, this book can help.

Making Every Day Count is a book of daily readings, meaning there's a page for every day of the year (including February 29 for Leap Year). Each reading begins with a *quotation* meant to get you interested and start you thinking. A brief *essay* goes deeper into the topic; you might find questions to consider, tips to try, examples, or a story related to the quotation. An *I-statement* suggests an action you might take, a decision you might make, or another way to use these ideas in your everyday life.

This is *your* book; you can use it any way you want. The easiest and most obvious is to read each day's entry at the start of the day. Then you can think it over during the day, and you'll have time to try out the I-statement. If you'd rather read it before you go to bed at night, read the next day's entry and sleep on it. If you want to share this book with others, you could ask your teacher to read each day's entry to the whole class. Or maybe you could read it over the morning announcements. Or what about reading it with a parent, a sibling, or a friend?

Some of these readings will reinforce things you already know or do. Some might be new to you. And some might raise questions you can't answer for yourself, or spotlight a problem you can't solve on your own. When this happens, please talk with an adult you trust and respect. This might be a parent, another relative, a teacher, a neighbor, a youth group leader, a religious leader, a mentor, a friend's parent, the school counselor, or someone else you know.

As you read your way through the year, you might want to keep a journal (if you don't already). Record your thoughts and ideas, questions and dreams, mistakes and successes. Then you'll have a record of your personal growth—and proof that you're making every day count.

"Life is a big canvas.
Throw all the paint on it you can."

Danny Kaye

Forget about making New Year's resolutions. (Can you name two people who actually *keep* their resolutions?) Instead, paint the canvas of your life with hopes, dreams—and goals. Begin by listing your goals for this year. Where would you like to be a year from now? What do you want to accomplish by then? Find something to write on or in (a piece of paper, your daily planner or journal, a notebook you use every day), go someplace quiet where you won't be interrupted, and start writing.

 **TODAY**

I'll list my goals for this year.

✳ JANUARY 2 ✳

"The more specific your goals are,
the more likely you are to achieve them—
and to know when you've achieved them."

Judy Galbraith and Jim Delisle

Are you excited about your goals and eager to get started, or worried that you can't possibly succeed? If you're worried, maybe it's because your goals are too vague. *Example:* "I'll make new friends" sounds good, but it's not specific enough. Instead, you might try: "I'll join the hiking club because Joe belongs and I'd like to be his friend. Also, I enjoy hiking." Take time to review and, if necessary, revise your goals. Make each one as precise as you can.

 TODAY

I'll set specific goals.

✳ JANUARY 3 ✳

"The way to success:
First, have a clear goal, not a fuzzy one."

Norman Vincent Peale

A religious leader, lecturer, radio broadcaster, syndicated newspaper columnist, and author of *The Power of Positive Thinking* (among other books), Norman Vincent Peale knew all about goal setting and success. He went on to say: "Sharpen this goal until it becomes specific and clearly defined in your conscious mind. Hold it there until it seeps into your unconscious. Surround this goal constantly with positive thoughts and faith. Give it positive follow-through. That is the way success is achieved."

 **TODAY**

I'll think positively about my goals.

✳ JANUARY 4 ✳

"It seems obvious that the first rule
of life is to have a good time."

Brendan Gill

When you're listing your goals for the year, don't forget to include the fun stuff—your hobbies, interests, friends, and things you most enjoy. Don't think of these as rewards for reaching your "real" goals; make them goals all by themselves—things you write down, plan for, and achieve. Would you like to go dancing every Saturday night? Add it to your list. Want to learn more about computer animation? Make it a goal.

 **TODAY**

I'll include enjoyment in my goals.

✳ JANUARY 5 ✳

"The reason most people never reach their
goals is that they don't define them,
or ever seriously consider them
as believable or achievable."

Denis Waitley

Ask your parents (or other adults you know) what their goals were when they were your age. Did they reach their goals? If they did, invite them to tell you about it. You may hear stories of hard work, dedication, planning, and luck. If they didn't reach their goals, try to find out why. Maybe their goals were vague or unrealistic; maybe they never really believed in them. A goal you don't believe in is nothing but a wish.

 **TODAY**

**I'll believe in my goals.
And I'll believe I can reach them.**

✳ JANUARY 6 ✳

"Rome was not built in one day."

John Heywood

This old saying appeared in a book that was printed in 1546. It was probably already a cliché, but it was true then and it's still true. If you haven't finished listing your goals for the year…no problem. Goal setting is a process that lasts a lifetime. If you're just starting, go slowly. Don't set too many goals at once. Don't try to juggle too many at the same time. You might need to revise your goals as circumstances change. You might have to give up some goals along the way. Be flexible and don't get discouraged. Above all, don't give up!

 TODAY

**I'll remind myself that
goal setting is a process.**

✳ JANUARY 7 ✳

"The victory of success
is half won when one gains the habit
of setting goals and achieving them."

Og Mandino

Research has shown that it takes two to three weeks to form a new habit. To make goal setting a habit, do it every day (weekends, too!) for 14 days and preferably 21. This will get you where you want to go and also make everyday life more meaningful. Og Mandino (author, salesman, and expert on human nature) went on to say: "Even the most tedious chore will become endurable as you parade through each day convinced that every task, no matter how menial or boring, brings you closer to fulfilling your dreams."

 **T O D A Y**

I'll make goal setting a habit.

✳ JANUARY 8 ✳

"Advice for life: 1. Love yourself.
2. Be yourself. 3. Always keep a journal."

Jessica Wilber

Keeping a personal journal is like creating your own treasure map. As you write, you'll discover a wealth of information about yourself: your aspirations, your secret wishes, and your hopes and dreams. These are your truest treasures.

 **TODAY**

**I'll start a journal or write
in my current journal.**

✳ JANUARY 9 ✳

"When I look at the future,
it's so bright, it burns my eyes."

Oprah Winfrey

What does the future hold for you? *Everything*...if you want it to. Dreams don't come true by accident; you have to make them happen. How? Work hard. Have hope. Be persistent. Keep faith. And above all, believe that the future is bright.

 **TODAY**

**I'll imagine my future
in a positive light.**

"If a window of opportunity appears,
don't pull down the shade."

Tom Peters

An opportunity might be anything at all. A chance to meet someone, go somewhere, learn something, or experience something new. A job offer, a mentorship, an invitation to join a club, take a class, give a speech, or climb a mountain...you never know. Sometimes it's easier to say "No thanks" or "Maybe another time," especially if you're not sure you'll enjoy what's being offered—or there's no guarantee you'll succeed. Try putting aside your doubts and fears. If you need encouragement, talk to a good friend or a trusted adult.

 **TODAY**

I'll take advantage of an opportunity.

> "If you want a quality, act as if you already had it. Try the 'as if' technique."
>
> *William James*

If you want to be a person of character—someone with strong values and beliefs—act like one. If you want to be honest, responsible, trustworthy, caring, positive, confident, fair, sincere, courageous, creative, or whatever, act as if you already are. If you want to be excited about school, put on an excited face and attitude. Then keep it up. This technique is amazingly powerful. Try it for a few days (or longer) and see how you feel. Pay attention to how other people treat you. Do you notice a difference?

 **TODAY**

I'll act like someone who's

_____.

(fill in the blank)

"Good words are worth much,
and cost little."

George Herbert

What's the greatest gift you can give someone? A video game? Tickets to a concert? A new jacket? A million dollars? Presents are nice, but one of the best gifts you can give—kind words—won't cost you any money. Tell your mom you love her, give your brother a compliment, leave an anonymous note on a friend's locker saying "Have a great day!" or "Nice work in math!" If you've argued with someone, apologize so you'll both feel better. *Tip:* The more kind words you give, the more you'll receive.

 **TODAY**

I'll say a kind word to someone.

"I wish I had me to listen to
when I was 14."

Alanis Morissette

When Canadian singer-songwriter Alanis Morissette gives a live concert, audience members sing along. They know her songs by heart; they feel that her music speaks directly to them. Music can be a powerful force in your life. It can move you, inspire you, and make you feel you're not alone. It can raise your spirits when you're down, calm you when you're hyper, or boost your energy when you're blah. What music speaks directly to you? It might have lyrics, but it doesn't have to. Some melodies are songs without words.

 **TODAY**

I'll listen to music.

✳ JANUARY 14 ✳

"There's a certain level of confidence
and self-esteem that comes from knowing
for a fact that someone loves you."

Will Smith

Will Smith—television actor, rapper, movie star—knows for a fact that his parents love him. They separated when he was 13, but they're still a big part of his life. Their love has given him tremendous strength throughout the years. "It's not based on whether or not I break a window; it's not based on whether or not my homework's done. Just because I'm me, these people love me." Who loves you—just because you're you?

 **TODAY**

**I'll appreciate the people
who love me.**

✳ JANUARY 15 ✳

"You give but little when you give
of your possessions. It is when you give
of yourself that you truly give."

Kahlil Gibran

It's great to make a donation to a worthy cause, but what about volunteering your time? It's wonderful to drop off used clothing and toys at a homeless shelter, but what about spending an hour each week reading to or playing with the kids? It's terrific to collect canned items for a local food shelf, but what about serving meals in a soup kitchen? Come face-to-face with the people you're helping. It will open your eyes, change your perspective, and make your giving more meaningful.

 **TODAY**

I'll give of myself.

✳ JANUARY 16 ✳

"Procrastination is the art of
keeping up with yesterday."

Don Marquis

Are you a procrastinator? Then you know how this can mess up your life—and keep you from reaching your goals. Follow these steps to conquer procrastination:

1. Think about something you've been procrastinating about.
2. Think about how you feel because you haven't done it. (Sad? Afraid? Worried? Stressed? Disgusted?)
3. Think about how GREAT you'll feel when you finally do it.
4. Picture yourself doing it. See it in your mind. Think positively about it.
5. Do it now! Or as soon as you can—today. (If you can't do it all today, break it into steps.)

 **TODAY**

I'll do one thing I've been putting off.

✳ JANUARY 17 ✳

"If you keep saying things are going
to be bad you have a good chance
of being a prophet."

Isaac Bashevis Singer

Do you go through life waiting for bad things to happen and always expecting the worst? And when something goes wrong, do you say "I was right! I knew it wouldn't work out for me"? You've created a *self-fulfilling prophecy*—you've predicted your failure and perhaps even helped it happen. Try this instead: Predict that you'll succeed, then see what happens. If you do succeed, you can still say "I was right!"

 **TODAY**

I'll believe the best will happen.

✳ JANUARY 18 ✳

"I thought I'd like myself better
if I was skinnier, but now I know that
this is who I am. And that's okay,
because it's part of what makes me *me*."

Raina Lowell

Many people—adults and teens—start diets in January. They feel like they ate too much over the holidays or they're too fat, and they see the New Year as a fresh start. In fact, losing weight is one of the most common New Year's resolutions people make. Are you on a diet? If you are, ask yourself why. Are you actually overweight, or are you trying to live up to the images you see in magazines and on TV? Do you think you'll like yourself more if you're thinner, or that other people will like you more?

 **TODAY**

I'm fine the way I am.

❊ JANUARY 19 ❊

"Dieting isn't healthy.
Health comes from well-being."

Rene Russo

If you want to eat right and get healthy, know that *having a healthy diet* and *being on a diet* aren't the same. Being on a diet means depriving yourself of food, not eating healthy. Diets are dangerous (especially for teens), and *they don't work*. When you drastically limit your food intake, any weight you lose is from fluids and muscle tissue—not fat. Your body thinks you're starving it and reacts by hoarding fat and slowing the rate at which you burn calories. This makes it nearly impossible to lose an ounce—you're simply storing the fat you wanted to lose in the first place. What to do? Stop dieting and start exercising.

 **TODAY**

I'll respect my body and treat it well.

"I've failed over and over and over again
in my life. And that is why I succeed."

Michael Jordan

When Michael Jordan was a high school sophomore, he was cut from the varsity basketball team. Even as a superstar, he's missed shots and lost games. In 1993, he left basketball to play minor league baseball…not very well, as it turned out. (He went back to basketball in 1995.) He's enormously wealthy, popular, and famous throughout the world, but what Michael Jordan wants young people to know is this: "Don't be afraid to fail, because a lot of people have to fail to be successful."

 **TODAY**

I won't be afraid to fail.

✳ JANUARY 21 ✳

"We would sit there and talk for hours.
That's how we built up trust and
respect for each other."

Tiger Woods

Golf star Tiger Woods is describing his relationship with his father—a relationship that's famously close, and one Tiger credits with being critical to his success. When was the last time you sat and talked with one (or both) of your parents for hours…or minutes? In a recent study by Search Institute, nearly 20 percent of 6th–12th graders said they hadn't had a good conversation (lasting for at least ten minutes) with either one of their parents in more than a month.

 **TODAY**

I'll talk with my parents.

"Regret is an appalling waste of energy;
you can't build on it; it's only good
for wallowing in."

Katherine Mansfield

We all have regrets. Things we wished we'd said or done. Things we wished we hadn't said or done. Dwelling on or wallowing in your regret won't change things; it will only make you miserable. If you can do something specific to make things right (if it's not too late), then do it. If you can't, just let it go.

 **TODAY**

I'll let go of an old regret.

✳ JANUARY 23 ✳

"The invention of the teenager
was a mistake, in Miss Manners' opinion."

Judith Martin ("Miss Manners")

You might feel the same way as you're going through the changes, hormonal rages, stresses, messes, and frustrations of adolescence. Who invented this time of life anyway, and are they purposely messing with your mind or what? It may help to know that just about everyone feels like a freak during the teen years. (Comedian Carol Burnett once described adolescence as "one big walking pimple.") The ultimate challenge for you is to find and hold onto your true self, despite the ups and downs of puberty. Holding on will help you pull through.

 **TODAY**

I'll hold onto who I am.

"How we remember, what we remember,
and why we remember form the most
personal map of our individuality."

Christina Baldwin

Our minds are filled with memories that have been stored there since we were infants. Anything can trigger a memory: a familiar scene, voice, smell, sound, dream, or song. What's your favorite memory? Your least favorite? Who's the most memorable person in your life, and why? What's the earliest memory you have?

 **TODAY**

I'll spend time remembering.

"Focus 90 percent of your time
on solutions and only 10 percent
of your time on problems."

Anthony J. D'Angelo

When you focus mostly on problems, you soon feel helpless and hopeless. Your mind is filled with negative thoughts—*I can't do that. My life is awful. Why me? Poor me!* But when you focus on solutions, your mind is filled with possibilities. Problem solving stimulates your brain, boosts your creativity, and strengthens your self-esteem. You think in terms of positives, not negatives, and you don't have time to feel sorry for yourself. Even if you can't solve every problem you face, it's empowering to try.

 **TODAY**

I'll focus on solutions.

"Self-knowledge is the beginning
of self-improvement."

Spanish proverb

If you created a self-portrait, what would it reveal about you? Maybe you'd paint a huge canvas, using vivid colors to show that you love to make a statement. Or maybe you'd use watercolors and paint yourself in a landscape to show the world you're quiet and you enjoy the outdoors. Or you might illustrate yourself in a funny cartoon to reveal your sense of humor. Do a self-portrait, and don't worry if you're not artistic (you don't have to show it to anyone else). What do you discover about yourself?

 **TODAY**

I'll do a self-portrait.

"There are two ways of exerting
one's strength: one is pushing down,
the other is pulling up."

Booker T. Washington

Conflicts are part of life, but you can learn to resolve disagreements peacefully. It takes a strong person to reach out to someone during an argument and say "Let's figure out a way to solve this problem" or "Let's make up." Working out your differences with someone—by handling your anger, listening to the other person's point of view, even apologizing—can make you feel stronger and happier.

 **TODAY**

I'll be peaceful.

✳ JANUARY 28 ✳

"I work on instinct. It's my best adviser."

Diana, Princess of Wales

Instinct led Princess Diana to hug sick children, hold hands with lepers and AIDS patients, visit homeless shelters, and show compassion for all kinds of people. You may have similar instincts to reach out and help others. Follow them. Find out where and how you can do the most good. Ask a counselor, youth leader, or religious leader for suggestions. You may not be a princess (or a prince), but you can make a big difference in someone else's life.

 **TODAY**

I'll follow my instincts.

"When you have a great and difficult task,
something perhaps almost impossible,
if you only work a little at a time, every day
a little, suddenly the work will finish itself."

Isak Dinesen

If you're facing a difficult task that seems overwhelming (a science fair project, for example), break it down into smaller, more manageable steps. First, make a list of all you need to do. Next, write down when each task needs to be completed. Then use a calendar or daily planner to determine what you'll need to do each day to stay on track. If you follow your plan, you'll finish the work in no time. (In the words of Benjamin Franklin, "Little strokes fell great oaks.")

 **TODAY**

**I'll break down a big task
into small steps.**

✳ JANUARY 30 ✳

"Notice the difference between
what happens when a man says
to himself, 'I have failed three times,' and
what happens when he says, 'I'm a failure.'"

S.I. Hayakawa

Say each pair of sentences to yourself and see how you feel:

"I have failed three times."   "I'm a failure."

"I don't understand the assignment." "I'm stupid."

"I don't have a date for the dance."   "I'm a loser."

The sentences on the left are statements of fact; the ones on the right are labels. Those on the left leave room for change—you can (1) try again, (2) get help, (3) go with a friend. Those on the right give you no way out. Labels are limiting, so avoid them!

 **TODAY**

I won't label myself.

"Learning is kind of the maximum
expression of being human. You try
to learn to grow and be more."

Gary Paulsen

*Why am I here? Why are any of us here? What is the
meaning of life?* These are big questions and worth
asking. So…who has the answers? The answers lie
within *you.* Your life isn't an accident; you're here for a
reason—a purpose. But it's up to you to find your purpose and to give your life meaning. You can start by
asking yourself questions like these: *What do I want
to accomplish? What are my goals and dreams? What
steps do I need to take to make my dreams come true?*
Discovering your purpose helps you make the most of
your life.

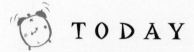 **TODAY**

I'll develop a sense of purpose.

❖ FEBRUARY 1 ❖

"Time is life. It is irreversible and
irreplaceable. To waste your time is to
waste your life, but to master your time is to
master your life and make the most of it."

Alan Lakein

If you have trouble managing your time, you can do
something about it. Here's one way to start:

1. Make a written Things to Do list. Keep it short
   and simple so you don't get overwhelmed; you
   might limit it to 5 things you need to do.

2. Once you've written down your 5 things,
   number them from 1 to 5, starting with the
   most important.

3. Look at #1 on your list. Is this something you
   can do today? If not—if it's too big or
   complicated—break it down into steps. Then
   number the steps and do the first step today.

 **TODAY**

I'll make a Things to Do list.

◆ FEBRUARY 2 ◆

"Behold the turtle. He makes progress
only when he sticks his neck out."

James Bryant Conant

A frightened turtle is immobilized. With its head hidden and feet tucked in, the turtle stands in place until danger passes. Are you like a turtle hiding in its shell? Fearful of new faces and places? Scared of trying new things? Afraid to stick your neck out? If you are, talk to an adult you trust. You can learn to come out of your shell.

 **TODAY**

**I'll talk about my fears
with someone I trust.**

❧ FEBRUARY 3 ❧

> "I care not what others think of what I do,
> but I care very much about what I think
> of what I do. That is character!"

Theodore Roosevelt

You want to join the chess club, but you're sure your friends will make fun of you. You've considered writing an editorial for the school paper, but you're afraid to express your opinion ("What will people *think?*"). You hate playing the oboe, but your dad plays the oboe, and you're worried that quitting will let him down. Instead of worrying about what *other* people think of you, ask yourself what *you* think of you. What do you want in life?

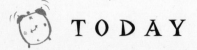 **TODAY**

I'll focus on what *I* think of me.

❖ FEBRUARY 4 ❖

"The excursion is the same
when you go looking for your sorrow
as when you go looking for your joy."

Eudora Welty

When you're an optimist, you think positively. You believe that good things will happen. You hope for the best. You look for your joy. Positive thoughts can rev you up and give you momentum. They help you move forward…and enjoy the journey.

 **TODAY**

I'll think like an optimist.

◆ FEBRUARY 5 ◆

"Use what talent you possess:
the woods would be very silent if no
birds sang except those that sang best."

Henry Van Dyke

So what if you don't get the lead in the play. Are you in the cast? You can still play a role—and have fun. Where would an opera singer be without the chorus? A solo violinist without the orchestra? A school newspaper editor without a staff? A student council president without a council? Santa without the elves? You get the picture. Now go out and do something you enjoy—and don't worry about being a star.

 **TODAY**

I'll find ways to use my talents.

❧ FEBRUARY 6 ❧

"Thank God for unanswered prayers."

Ben Affleck

He costarred in *Good Will Hunting* (and shared the Academy Award for Best Original Screenplay with Matt Damon); you might have seen him in *Armageddon* and other movies. But before Ben Affleck was a star, he was out of work and broke. One day he went to an audition for *Beverly Hills 90210*—and blew it. The casting director called his agent and yelled "He'll *never* be on *Beverly Hills 90210!*" Today Affleck is glad he didn't get the part. (Sometimes it's best *not* to get what you want because something better is waiting.)

TODAY

I'll be grateful for a time when I didn't get what I wanted.

❦ FEBRUARY 7 ❦

"The direct use of force is such a poor
solution to any problem, it is generally
employed only by small children
and large nations."

David Friedman

Violence is *never* the solution to a problem. There is
always a better way. Tips to try:

- Talk about small conflicts before they become
  big problems.
- When you're angry, talk more *quietly* than usual.
- Many conflicts fade away when people really
  listen to each other. Look at other people when
  they're talking; acknowledge what they're saying;
  don't interrupt, but ask questions if you need
  more information.

 **TODAY**

I'll solve a problem peacefully.

"Peace is not a passive but an active
condition, not a negation but an affirmation.
It is a gesture as strong as war."

Mary Roberts Rinehart

Here are more ways to solve problems peacefully:

- If you're too angry to talk (or the other person is too angry to listen), go to a quiet place and write about how angry you are. Or go for a walk, run, or bike ride.
- Ask people you respect how they solve problems peacefully. Do they have any tips to share with you? Any stories about their own experiences?
- Spend time each day in quiet thought. Get to know yourself and your feelings. Figure out what makes you tick…and what makes you want to explode. Come up with alternatives to exploding.

 TODAY

**I'll ask someone I respect
for problem-solving tips.**

❖ FEBRUARY 9 ❖

"Do all the good you can,
By all the means you can,
In all the ways you can,
In all the places you can,
At all the times you can."

Anonymous

When you *do* good, you *feel* good. Reach out to someone in need, lend a hand in your community, volunteer at a homeless shelter or nursing home, or take steps to improve the environment. You can do your part to make the world a better place.

 **TODAY**

I'll do a good deed.

"Dreams are illustrations…from the book
your soul is writing about you."

Marsha Norman

Many artists, poets, musicians, scientists, and inventors have said their nightly dreams sparked their creativity or led them to amazing discoveries. Dreams are a rich source of information about ourselves, our lives, and our deepest thoughts and feelings. What do your dreams tell you? If you don't usually remember your dreams, try this tip: Keep a Dream Journal and something to write with next to your bed. Each morning, *as soon as you wake up*, write down everything you recall about last night's dreams. Dreams start fading from your memory almost immediately, so don't wait until later to do this.

TODAY

**I'll think about what I dreamed
last night. Are my dreams trying
to tell me something?**

❦ FEBRUARY 11 ❦

"I remember that I was never able
to get along at school. I was always
at the foot of the class."

Thomas Alva Edison

Is school a chore or a bore for you? In class, do you twiddle your thumbs, catch a quick nap, or watch the clock s-l-o-w-l-y tick away the minutes? You're not the only one. Many students sometimes feel confused or unchallenged at school. If your schoolwork seems dull, unclear, or pointless, talk to your teacher. Don't be embarrassed to say "I feel lost" or "I wish I felt more challenged." Teachers are there to help, so let them. For tips on talking to teachers, see pages 284–285. (P.S. Today is Edison's birthday.)

 **TODAY**

I'll talk to my teacher.

❦ FEBRUARY 12 ❦

"Are anybody's parents typical?"

Madeleine L'Engle

Do your parents seem totally weird? (If they don't right now, they will before too long. Believing your parents are aliens is a normal part of growing up and becoming independent.) Instead of wishing you could trade them or upgrade them, give it a rest. So what if your mom dresses funny or your dad is obsessed with championship bowling. Maybe they're not the coolest, and maybe they're embarrassing to be around. It's possible that your parents have changed, but more likely that your *perception* of them has changed.

 **TODAY**

**I'll love my parents
just the way they are.**

"An aim in life is the only fortune
worth finding."

Jacqueline Kennedy Onassis

Adults have probably asked you "What do you want to be when you grow up?" or "What do you plan to do with your life?" As children, we see a world of possibilities: firefighter, astronaut, artist, athlete, animal trainer. As we grow older, the possibilities may narrow: "I'd like to be a vet, but I'm not good at science," "I'll never be a great artist, so why even try?" These fears and doubts are self-limiting—and self-defeating. If there's something you *really* want to do, start finding ways to do it. It's not too early…or too late.

TODAY

I'll think about my
dream job or career.

❦ FEBRUARY 14 ❦

"When first we fall in love, we feel
that we know all there is to know
about life, and perhaps we are right."

Mignon McLaughlin

Today is St. Valentine's Day. Long ago, people believed that birds chose their mates on this day. You probably haven't yet met the person you'll want to spend your life with…or maybe you have and you don't know it. (It's possible that your grandparents were childhood sweethearts. Ask them!) Even when you're not in love, it's fun to exchange Valentine's cards with your friends. As a day-brightener, you might send a secret Valentine to someone who's new in school, at home sick, or in need of cheering up for any reason.

 **TODAY**

I'll send someone a secret Valentine.

❖ FEBRUARY 15 ❖

"Strangers are friends that you
have yet to meet."

Roberta Lieberman

Having a pen pal (or several) is a great way to feel connected to other people, cultures, and parts of the world. You can get a pen pal by writing or calling: International Pen Friends (IPF), 500 University Avenue, #2415, Honolulu, HI 96826; (809) 949-5000. If you're online, you probably know that the Internet links people young and old all over the whole world. Contact IPF on the Web at: *www.pen-pals.net/ipf/ipf.html*

 TODAY

**I'll take the first step toward
getting a pen pal.**

❦ FEBRUARY 16 ❦

"If life is a bowl of cherries,
what am I doing in the pits?"

Erma Bombeck

Depression is the pits. When you're depressed, you're overcome by painful feelings such as sadness, anger, hopelessness, guilt, and loneliness. You may also have physical reactions like headaches, fatigue, nausea, or sleeping problems. Bev Cobain, a psychiatric nurse who works with teens, describes depression as feeling like "a deep, dark hole." The first step toward climbing out is determining if you might be depressed. Ask yourself if you've been experiencing some of the mental and physical symptoms described here. Have these symptoms bothered you for two weeks or more? You might try keeping a Feelings Journal for a few days or a week so you notice any changes in your emotions.

 **TODAY**

I'll start a Feelings Journal.

❧ FEBRUARY 17 ❧

"The basic trouble with depression
is that it's so depressing."

Miss Piggy

If you've been feeling sad and hopeless for a while,
and you think you might be depressed, talk with an
adult you trust. You may be reluctant to confide in
someone, but *it helps*. If you're not sure what to say, you
can start with something like this: "I'm feeling really
bad. I think I might be depressed." If you can, be more
specific about how you're feeling: sad, afraid, hopeless,
sick, angry, tired all the time. Or you might just say
"I feel like nothing matters anymore. I may need some
help." You'll probably be relieved to get your feelings out
in the open.

 **TODAY**

**I'll share my feelings
with an adult I trust.**

"Our feelings are our most genuine
paths to knowledge."

Audre Lorde

Overcoming depression (or any other emotional difficulty) takes time and effort. As you work on healing, you might wonder why life has to be so tough. You might even ask "Why me?" Instead of focusing on the obstacle, think about how much stronger you're becoming each day. The challenge you're facing is helping you to learn and grow. As you get well, you'll also discover what you need to do to *stay* well. This knowledge can help you for the rest of your life.

 **TODAY**

**I'll focus on how a challenge
is working *for* me.**

♦ FEBRUARY 19 ♦

"Know what you love and do what you love.
If you don't do what you love,
you're just wasting your time."

Billy Joel

Doing what you love can lead to all sorts of wonderful feelings—excitement, awe, joy, satisfaction, pride. On the other hand, *not* doing what you love can leave you feeling discouraged, angry, unhappy, and unfulfilled. Doing what you love is vital to your emotional health.

 **TODAY**

I'll do something I love.

"I have made mistakes, but I have never made
the mistake of claiming I never made one."

James G. Bennet

Everyone makes mistakes, but not everyone comes
clean. Here are four good reasons to admit it when you
goof up:

1. You feel better. There's a load off your mind.
2. It's easier and less time-consuming than covering
   up, denying, lying, or making excuses.
3. Once the mistake is out in the open, you can
   start doing something about it.
4. People will admire you. So few people admit
   their mistakes that you'll stand out as a shining
   example of honesty and courage.

 **TODAY**

I'll admit a mistake.

❖ FEBRUARY 21 ❖

> "Whoever gossips to you
> will gossip about you."
>
> *Spanish proverb*

Tracy tells you that Tina has a problem at home—her parents are always fighting. Marcus says that James was caught shoplifting. Allan is sure he saw Ben smoking a cigarette at the park. Stories, rumors, hearsay, gossip— they can rule your life if you let them. Never assume that someone is sharing a secret only with you—or that he or she will keep your confidences. Before you jump to conclusions, get the facts. And keep yourself out of the gossip loop.

 **TODAY**

**I won't listen to gossip—
and I won't spread it.**

"Turn your wounds into wisdom."

Oprah Winfrey

Suffering, hurts, disappointments, pain, mistakes....
These are wounds we all experience at some point in
our lives. Wounds can be our teachers, our guides, our
healers. We can learn from them. Let a mistake lead you
to the right way to do something next time. Allow a
painful experience to open your eyes to the good things
you have. Know that suffering can help you appreciate
the fragile beauty of life.

TODAY

I'll let a hurt heal.

◆ FEBRUARY 23 ◆

"To make the right choices in life, you have to get in touch with your soul. To do this, you need to experience solitude, which most people are afraid of, because in the silence you hear the truth and know the solutions."

Deepak Chopra

Where can you go to find solitude? Your room? The public library? A park? A museum? The sanctuary in a house of worship? Don't be afraid to be alone. It may take getting used to—especially if you're usually around friends and family members, with music playing or the TV blaring. It may seem strange and boring at first. Be patient. Give it time. You might bring your journal and write about how you feel—and what you discover about yourself.

 **TODAY**

I'll spend time alone.

◆ FEBRUARY 24 ◆

"Problems are my friends."

Milton Glaser

Twelve-year-old Aja Henderson of Baton Rouge, Louisiana, noticed a problem. A lot of her friends and the neighborhood children didn't have anyone to take them to the library. Many parents worked, and by the time they got home, the libraries were closed. So Aja opened her own library—in the den of her home. Today her library has more than 3,000 titles, and young children, teenagers, and adults all use it. The library doesn't have any set hours, and it's open seven days a week.

 **TODAY**

**I'll notice a problem
and come up with a solution.**

"To change and to change for the better
are two different things."

German proverb

"You've changed! I hardly recognize you anymore."
Have your parents ever said this to you? (If they have, it
was probably during an argument.) As a teen, you're
growing and changing quickly, and your appearance,
tastes, ideas, and view of the world may change on a
daily basis. You're figuring out who you are, and you're
developing a sense of self. Don't be surprised if your
parents or other people in your life start wondering
where the child they used to know has gone.
Meanwhile, ask yourself if the changes they're seeing in
you are for the better.

 **TODAY**

**I'll pay attention to the changes
in myself. Are they mostly positive
or mostly negative?**

"Creativity shows its colors serendipitously.
You never know when it's going to arise
or what will awaken the wonderful beast."

Ken Vinton

You're standing in the shower, and suddenly an idea for a great story pops into your head. You're gazing out the window, lost in a daydream, and unexpectedly come up with an amazing invention. You never know when or where an incredible thought will surface. But if you give your mind time to wander freely, as it does when you're relaxed or daydreaming, creativity might show its colors…out of the blue.

 **TODAY**

I'll let my mind wander.

❖ FEBRUARY 27 ❖

"No one can say of his house,
'There is no trouble here.'"

Oriental proverb

Every family has problems. A family meeting is a great way to bring problems into the open and find solutions. Try these family meeting tips:

1. Set a time and date for the meeting. Make sure it's convenient for everyone.
2. State the *main* problem you're having. Stick to the facts, don't exaggerate, and don't bring up a lot of other problems or gripes.
3. Let everyone tell their side of the story. Listen.
4. Invite other family members to offer suggestions for how to solve the problem.
5. Agree to try one of the suggestions, and give it a good chance.

 **TODAY**

I'll suggest a family meeting.

❦ FEBRUARY 28 ❦

"The longer I live, the more I realize
the impact of attitude on life."

Charles Swindoll

Swindoll—president of Dallas Theological Seminary, author, and speaker on *Insight for Living* (a radio ministry)—goes on to say: "Attitude to me is more important than facts. It is more important than the past, than education, than money, than circumstances, than failures, than success, than what other people think or say or do. It is more important than appearance, gift, or skill…. The remarkable thing is we have a choice every day regarding the attitude we will embrace for that day…. We are in charge of our attitudes."

 **TODAY**

**I'll choose my attitude
wisely and carefully.**

❖ FEBRUARY 29 ❖

"Above all, try something."

Franklin Delano Roosevelt

If you're reading this on February 29, it must be Leap Year—that bonus day that comes once every four years. It's a perfect day to take a leap and try something new. Forget your usual excuses—"I'm not athletic enough" (smart enough, good enough, etc.) or "It's not worth it" or whatever you tell yourself when you're anxious, worried that you won't succeed, or just plain lazy. Do something you've never done before. Write a poem for a literary magazine, eat sushi, sign up for guitar lessons, volunteer at a nursing home, paint a portrait, or ride the biggest roller coaster at an amusement park. Take a chance—*try something.*

 **TODAY**

I'll take a leap.

MARCH 1

"Knowing what you want is
the first step toward getting it."

Mae West

If you have goals you'd like to pursue, try writing them in a Goals Journal. Record each goal in as much detail as possible. Write about why you want to accomplish it, how you'll pursue it, and when you think you can reasonably reach it. Each time you take a step toward a goal, write it in your journal. If you experience a setback, note that, too. This is a helpful way to measure your progress, anticipate any problems, and stay inspired.

 **TODAY**

I'll start a Goals Journal.

⊚ MARCH 2 ⊚

*"If you want a place in the sun,
you've got to put up with a few blisters."*

Abigail Van Buren ("Dear Abby")

At some point in your life, you'll do something that puts you in the spotlight. Maybe you'll write an article for your school paper, perform on stage, display your art, win a school election, or become the leader of a club or organization. You'll have a chance to express yourself and earn the recognition you deserve. It's possible, however, that some people won't react favorably to what you do. You may receive a bad review or be criticized for your efforts. Don't let this stop you from enjoying your place in the sun.

TODAY

**I'll remember the good things
people have said about me.**

◎ MARCH 3 ◎

"Everyone is wounded in some way.
Those of us who have found the means
to begin healing need to reach out
and help those who are still hurting."

Bev Cobain

Is someone you know—a sibling, friend, or class-mate—struggling with personal problems? Maybe you suspect he or she is unhappy, depressed, even suicidal. You can help. Ask a trusted adult for information and advice. (Seeking help doesn't mean you're betraying the person who needs it.) If you can't find someone to talk to, call a crisis hotline. The Covenant House Nineline is available 24 hours a day at 1-800-999-9999. If you're on the Web, you can go to: *www.nineline.org*

 **TODAY**

I'll help someone in need.

☺ MARCH 4 ☺

> "To be quite oneself
> one must first waste a little time."
>
> *Elizabeth Bowen*

If you're feeling stressed out, overwhelmed, and stretched too thin, maybe it's because you're over-committed. Many teens fill their lives with obligations—homework, chores, part-time jobs, extracurricular activities, clubs, volunteering. You need to make time to *waste* time—hanging out with friends, reading, watching videos, or just sitting and doing absolutely nothing. Especially for someone with a busy schedule, wasted time isn't really "wasted." It's time your brain and body need to relax and recover—time *you* need to be yourself.

 **TODAY**

I'll waste a little time.

"Self-esteem is the reputation
we acquire with ourselves."

Nathaniel Branden

Psychologist, educator, and author Alex J. Packer says this about self-esteem: "Some adults believe that the way to build self-esteem is by looking in a mirror and repeating self-congratulatory mantras. They teach kids to tell themselves 'I'm great at math, I'm lovable and good.' But this is just a mind trick. *The way to build genuine self-esteem is by doing esteemable things.* Care, give, treat others with kindness and tolerance, be honest but gentle with yourself, do the best you can in the things that really matter. You'll build your self-esteem—and it will be genuine and deserved."

 **TODAY**

I'll do something esteemable.

"It is wise to direct your anger towards problems—not people; to focus your energies on answers—not excuses."

William Arthur Ward

You're angry at your parents because they won't let you go out on Friday. So you yell at them and call them mean and unfair…and now you're grounded for a week. When you approach people in anger, you create new problems. Try these tips for talking to people when you're steamed:

1. Wait to talk until you're feeling more calm.
2. Talk more softly than usual.
3. Don't accuse or blame.
4. If you can't reach a solution, agree to meet later and try again.
5. Admit your role in the problem. Don't make excuses.

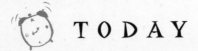 **TODAY**

I won't speak in anger.

MARCH 7

"If you have knowledge,
let others light their candles in it."

Margaret Fuller

Is there something you're an expert on? Computers? Cats? Cars? The stars? There are people who would love to learn from you. You might mentor a younger child in your neighborhood or community. Volunteer at a school, religious organization, community center, library, or nursing home. Join a service group that needs your expertise. Be a tutor. Or share your knowledge in other ways. Don't keep it to yourself; spread it around. You'll help others...and you'll feel good about yourself.

 **TODAY**

**I'll find ways to share
my knowledge with others.**

MARCH 8

"Pray before sleep, or read a great poem.
Sacred words will clear your crowded mind."

Judith Ortiz Cofer

Sleep is your body's chance to relax and renew itself.
If you have trouble winding down before bed
each night, you might try doing something that calms
you. You can pray, read, breathe deeply, write in your
journal, or think serene, quiet thoughts—whatever
makes you feel peaceful.

 **TODAY**

I'll clear my mind before I sleep.

"Too often we underestimate the power of
a touch, a smile, a kind word, a listening ear,
an honest compliment, or the smallest act
of caring, all of which have the potential
to turn a life around."

Leo Buscaglia

Known as "The Ambassador of Love," Leo Buscaglia
spent his life teaching people about love—in his lec-
tures, public television appearances, and books. He
hugged more people than anyone could count. He lived
his belief that small acts of caring could change lives.
You might want to read one of his books or watch one
of his videos (try the public library). Or see what happens when you treat people with kindness and love.

 **TODAY**

I'll touch someone's life.

⊙ MARCH 10 ⊙

"Life can do a really sharp turn on you
all of a sudden, and I always expect that."

Shania Twain

Country singer Shania Twain grew up in poverty. When she was 22, her parents were killed in a car crash, and she came home to raise her younger siblings. Her first album went almost unnoticed; her second won a Grammy Award and sold more than 9 million copies. Shania's life has been full of sharp turns, both bad and good. You can't predict what will happen in your life, but you can try to be prepared for whatever happens. When you're making plans, always have a "plan B"—a backup you can use if your original doesn't work out.

 **TODAY**

I'll make a plan—and a plan B.

"Bloom where you're planted."

Mary Engelbreit

Many people fall into the trap of believing that their "real" life is temporarily on hold or out of reach. They tell themselves that once they've reached a certain age or set of circumstances, their life will truly begin. Do you tell yourself that once you can drive, your life will really begin? Or that when you hit 18, everything will change and you'll start living the life you were meant to? (And that nothing counts until then?) Why not enjoy who you are and where you are at this very moment? According to Richard Carlson, "There's no better time to be happy than right now. If not now, when?"

 **TODAY**

I'll believe that happiness is something I can have right now.

MARCH 12

"I wanted to change my name
to Doris or Maggie growing up."

Ming-Na Wen

If you could change just one thing about yourself, what would it be? Your height? Your weight? Your nose? Your hair? Your name? Ming-Na Wen was born in Macau, China, but grew up in Mt. Lebanon, Pennsylvania, where her name stuck out like a sore thumb. She left her name alone, and today millions of people have seen it in the credits for TV programs and movies. In 1998, she was the voice of the lead character in Disney's animated film *Mulan*. And it's safe to assume that she's glad she never changed her name.

 **TODAY**

I like myself the way I am.

◎ MARCH 13 ◎

"I've learned that if you want your dreams
to come true, you've just got to be able to take
the misses with the hits."

Janeane Garofalo

Even the best-loved comedians can tell a joke that bombs. And the world's greatest singers sometimes sing a note off-key. Actors flub their lines, and dancers fall on their face. Sometimes you miss; sometimes you hit. The secret is to keep trying. Don't let a setback discourage you from pursuing your dreams.

 **TODAY**

**I'll identify one obstacle I'm facing—
and a way to overcome it.**

"Courage is not the absence of fear,
but rather the judgment that something
else is more important than fear."

Ambrose Redmoon

It takes courage to speak out against injustice, to stick up for a friend, to take an unpopular viewpoint, to go against the tide and stand apart from the crowd. You risk being picked on, excluded, labeled, even (in some cases) beat up. When is it worth it? That depends on what matters to you. In your mind, based on your values and beliefs, what's more important than fear? You might want to think this through, even write about it in your journal. The next time your courage is tested, you'll know what to do.

 **TODAY**

I'll be courageous.

◎ MARCH 15 ◎

"It's kind of fun to do the impossible."

Walt Disney

In 1923, Walt Disney opened his own animated cartoon studio in Los Angeles. In 1937, he released the first ever full-length cartoon feature film, *Snow White*. In 1955, he opened a family theme park, Disneyland. He did many supposedly impossible things during his lifetime—and had fun along the way. If you've ever *not* pursued a goal because others labeled it impossible, maybe it's time to give it a try.

 **TODAY**

**I'll do something I've
always wanted to do.**

⊚ MARCH 16 ⊚

> "There are always two choices,
> two paths to take. One is easy.
> And its only reward is that it's easy."
>
> *Anonymous*

Jess blew off studying for her big English test because she didn't want to miss the latest episodes of her favorite must-see TV shows. In the morning, she was too tired to cram, and she pretended to be sick. She couldn't believe how easy it was to fool her mom into letting her stay home all day watching soaps. But when Jess went back to school, she learned she had to take a make-up test as soon as possible. Meanwhile, everyone else in class had moved on to the next assignment—and Jess had to work extra hard to catch up.

 **TODAY**

I won't take the easy way out.

"I've always had a vision for myself."

Barbara Smith

Barbara Smith was the first African-American woman to appear on the cover of *Mademoiselle.* Today she hosts her own TV show, writes books, owns restaurants, and is known as a stylesetter and an expert on entertaining. Years ago, when she was thinking of starting a restaurant, friends advised her not to; it seemed too stereotyped, like Aunt Jemima in the kitchen. But Barbara Smith knew what she wanted to do, and she did it.

TODAY

I'll have a vision for myself.

◎ MARCH 18 ◎

"No matter how much pressure you feel
at work, if you could find ways to relax
for at least five minutes every hour,
you'd be more productive."

Dr. Joyce Brothers

Can you relax at a moment's notice—anytime, anywhere? If not, this is a skill you need. It restores your
energy, sharpens your focus, boosts your creativity, and
makes you more productive at work, at school, or
wherever you are. Try this relaxation technique:

1. Sit as comfortably as you can and close your eyes.
2. Take a long, slow, deep breath through your
   nose. Slowly count to 5 as you inhale.
3. Breathe out through your nose. Slowly count
   backwards from 5 as you exhale.
4. Repeat this slow, rhythmic breathing and
   counting for 3–5 minutes.

 **TODAY**

**I'll try to relax for brief periods
throughout the day.**

◎ MARCH 19 ◎

"Take rest; a field that has rested
gives a bountiful crop."

Ovid

Here's another quick and easy way to relax:
1. Sit as comfortably as you can.
2. Breathe deeply and naturally. In and out. In and out. Spend about a minute just breathing.
3. Think of a word or phrase—something totally stress-free. *Examples:* "blue sky," "soft rain," "pillow," "ocean."
4. Repeat your word or phrase over and over in your mind as you continue to breathe naturally. Eventually it will become meaningless—just sounds.
5. Do this for 3–5 minutes.

 **TODAY**

I'll practice a relaxation technique.

◎ MARCH 20 ◎

"The sweetest of all sounds is praise."

Anonymous

Doesn't it feel wonderful when someone gives you a compliment? Pass those good feelings on by paying a compliment yourself. Tell your teacher his tie looks great. Let your dad know that, in your eyes, he's the world's best cook. Send a note to your grandma saying how much everyone admires the sweater she sent you for your birthday. (Be genuine and sincere so people know you really *mean* what you say.) Try to compliment at least one person each day.

 **TODAY**

I'll give someone a compliment.

◎ MARCH 21 ◎

"A new idea is delicate. It can be killed
by a sneer or a yawn; it can be stabbed
to death by a joke or worried to death
by a frown on the right person's brow."

Charles Brower

If you've ever had an idea and been shot down, you
know how it feels. Don't do this to anyone else,
especially younger kids who look up to you. When you
have a new idea, share it with someone you trust—a
friend, teacher, parent, or mentor you can count on to
listen and offer *constructive* criticism. Constructive
criticism builds you up, gives specific suggestions
for making your idea even better, tells you honestly
when it won't work (and why), and encourages you to
keep trying.

 **TODAY**

**I'll seek and welcome
constructive criticism.**

"You cannot hold back a good laugh
any more than you can the tide.
Both are forces of nature."

William Rostler

Can you believe there's actually a day dedicated to goof-ing off? There is, and this is it. Today is National Goof-Off Day, created to celebrate loafing, being silly, and having fun. So tell some jokes. Be a clown. Laugh and make others do the same. Kick back and relax. Just for today, *be* rather than *do*.

 **TODAY**

I'll goof off.

⊚ MARCH 23 ⊚

"No pressure, no diamonds."

Mary Case

Deep beneath the earth's surface, a chunk of carbon undergoes tremendous pressure and heat…and crystallizes into the world's most precious stone (and hardest substance). When you're feeling overwhelmed by expectations, responsibilities, and too much stress, remember this. You might emerge from an especially tough time with greater strength—and sparkle.

 **TODAY**

I'll become stronger under pressure.

"You have to let people know
now how you feel about them,
because you never know what'll happen."

Jennifer Lopez

When was the last time you said "I love you" to your mom or dad? Or the last time they said it to you? Maybe your family talks freely about feelings—and maybe not. Many people have a hard time expressing emotions. If your family is the silent type, make a few small moves and see what happens. Toss off a "Later! Love you!" as you race out the door. Or leave a note signed "XXOO." It's possible that your parents grew up without hearing "I love you" from *their* parents. They may need some training.

 **TODAY**

I'll let people I love know that I care.

◎ MARCH 25 ◎

"Art washes away from the soul
the dust of everyday life."

Pablo Picasso

Art has the power to lift you out of yourself and take you places you've never been. It can make you think, dream, and feel. If you live near an art museum, go there and wander around. Stop in front of pictures or sculptures that interest you. Give yourself time to absorb their colors, shapes, and energy. If you don't live near an art museum, visit a library and look through art books. *Tip:* To view art online, visit the WebMuseum at: *www.ibiblio.org/wm*

 **TODAY**

I'll make time to enjoy art.

"Suffering is also one of the ways
of knowing you're alive."

Jessamyn West

No matter how miserable you feel, no matter how rotten your life seems to be, at least you're alive! Some teens get caught in a downward spiral of negative thinking and hopelessness. They become so depressed and desperate that they consider suicide—or attempt suicide. And many actually kill themselves. *If you ever even think about committing suicide, get help immediately.* Look under "Suicide Prevention" in your local phone book for a hotline. Or contact the Covenant House Nineline (see page 63). Someone *will* listen; someone *will* help you.

 **TODAY**

I'll be glad I'm alive, no matter what.

⊙ MARCH 27 ⊙

"Hope is one of those things in life
you cannot do without."

LeRoy Douglas

Here's advice from someone who thought a lot about suicide as a teen: "Although there were many nights when I cried myself to sleep, I never woke up crying in the morning. At some point, I realized that *I always felt better in the morning*—maybe only a little, but enough to get me through another day. There will probably be times in your life (if there haven't been already) when you feel hopeless and lonely—maybe enough to consider suicide. When they happen, always promise yourself at least one more morning."

 **TODAY**

**I'll promise myself to never,
ever lose hope.**

"Who you are speaks so loudly
I can't hear what you're saying."

Ralph Waldo Emerson

"Do what I say, not what I do." People you know might have said this to you—parents, teachers, or other adults in your life. Usually they mean well; they want to steer you away from mistakes they've made. But the best way to guide is by setting a good example. Actions speak louder than words. Keep this in mind when you're around younger kids and anyone else you might influence. When your actions match your words—when you walk the walk *and* talk the talk—that's called having *integrity*.

 TODAY

I'll act with integrity.

MARCH 29

"Once you get over that peak of puberty,
you hit a nice stride."

Claire Danes

Body changes, squeaky voices, zits, awkwardness, embarrassment, mood swings.... Who invented puberty, and why is it so awful? The good news is: It won't last forever. No matter where you are in the process, you'll survive! Meanwhile, if you have questions about puberty, get answers. Ask your librarian to recommend a book or two. Talk to your school counselor. Talk to your parents, if they're willing. *Tip:* Your friends might not know much more than you do, so it's probably best to take your questions to an adult you trust.

 **TODAY**

**I'll get answers to
my questions about puberty.**

89

◎ MARCH 30 ◎

"You have to know what you're good at
and what you're bad at."

Dineh Mohajer

In 1995, Dineh Mohajer was a pre-med student. One day, when she couldn't find nail polish to match her pale blue sandals, she mixed up a batch in her bathroom sink. Three years later, she was running a nail polish company—Hard Candy—with $10 million in annual sales. Dineh realized that medical school wasn't for her, and she made a decision that put her life on a different track. You're probably not ready to make career choices, but it's never too soon to get a handle on what you're good at—and what you're not so good at.

 **TODAY**

I'll list my strengths and weaknesses.

◎ MARCH 31 ◎

> "Each day comes bearing its own gifts.
> Untie the ribbons."
>
> *Ruth Ann Schabacker*

What happens when someone gives you a gift? You probably can't wait to see what's inside. You're happy, excited, and full of anticipation. Imagine what life would be like if you greeted each day as a series of gifts, one after another, all day long. The sun shining in your window…sitting next to a friend on the bus…going to classes…lunch…coming home after school…watching TV…spending time with your family…getting teased by your sister…your safe, warm bed…all gifts. Give it a try.

 **TODAY**

**I'll be excited about the gifts
the day brings.**

"Among those whom I like or admire,
I can find no common denominator,
but among those whom I love, I can:
all of them make me laugh."

W.H. Auden

According to comedian Norm Crosby, an authority on the subject, "Laughter is good for your face!" It's also good for your body. Laughter increases your breathing rate, muscular activity, heart rate, and other functions. It makes you feel great inside and out. If you need a good laugh, help is available. Rent a funny movie, listen to a comedy CD or cassette, read the Sunday comics or a comic book, or memorize some jokes and share them with your friends. Giggling is good for you. (P.S. Since today is April Fool's Day, have fun making other people laugh, too.)

 **TODAY**

I'll laugh.

"The time to repair the roof is
when the sun is shining."

John F. Kennedy

Maybe your life is going really, really well right now.
You're getting along with your family and friends,
keeping up in school, having fun, and generally feeling
good about yourself. You can relax and just enjoy
things—or you can take this opportunity to fix something that needs fixing. Is there an old hurt or
misunderstanding you could resolve? A task you've
been avoiding and could do? A friendship you could
strengthen? A problem you could solve?

 **TODAY**

I'll fix something that needs fixing.

⚜ APRIL 3 ⚜

> "Never look down on anybody
> unless you're helping them up."
>
> *Jesse Jackson*

Homeless people could find homes if they really tried. People on welfare could get jobs if they weren't so lazy. And students who fail their classes ought to study harder...right? It's easy to look down on people when we don't know the circumstances of their lives. When we look down on them, we can dismiss their problems and not get involved. But what if Mother Teresa had looked down on the poor people dying in the streets of India?

 **TODAY**

I won't look down on anyone.

"I don't believe in pessimism. If something doesn't come up the way you want, forge ahead. If you think it's going to rain, it will."

Clint Eastwood

I know I'm going to lose the race. I'll flunk this test for sure. There's no way I can win the award. He won't go out with me. She won't like me. Negative thoughts like these prepare you for failure. On the other hand, positive thoughts prepare you for success. So why not think positively? Count on a sunny day. Believe in life's goodness. Expect to win.

 **TODAY**

I'll think positively.

"It takes less time to do a thing right
than explain why you did it wrong."

Henry Wadsworth Longfellow

You probably have certain chores you're expected to do at home. Do you try to get out of them, or just do them? Do you find shortcuts, make excuses, then end up having to do them over? If you do something right the first time, you'll avoid arguments and win your parents' trust and respect. You can apply Longfellow's wisdom to every part of your life—school, your job (if you have one), and other obligations (to your community, club, youth group, or congregation, for example). See for yourself.

TODAY

**I'll do something right
from start to finish.**

"We are what we repeatedly do."

Aristotle

If you sincerely want to break a bad habit—no matter what it is—*you can do it.* Start by naming the habit you'd like to break. Then figure out the steps you can take to free yourself. Write them in your journal or daily planner. If you need help, list the names of people you can turn to. *Tip:* Some habits are almost impossible to break without help—like smoking, using alcohol or other drugs, and overeating. Talk to an adult you trust and respect. Consider joining a support group; ask your school counselor for recommendations.

 **TODAY**

I'll take the first step toward breaking a bad habit.

"Compassion for our parents
is the true sign of maturity."

Anaïs Nin

Do you know what life has *really* been like for your parents? Making a home, supporting a family, and raising you (terrific as you are) probably hasn't been easy. Your parents may have gone through tough times you know nothing about. If you're comfortable asking (and they're comfortable telling), you might talk about this together. What has been especially difficult for them? Is there anything they would have done differently? What words of advice do they have for you?

TODAY

I'll be thankful for my parents—
and I'll tell them so.

⚜ APRIL 8 ⚜

"Do what you can, with what you have,
where you are."

Theodore Roosevelt

Matthew Green, age 17, has Crohn's disease, a chronic illness that affects his digestive system. When complications from the illness kept him out of school for several months, Matthew didn't waste time feeling sorry for himself. Instead, he decided to make the most of a bad situation. He started a Web site that offers help and hope for teens with Crohn's, and now thousands of young people benefit from Matthew's words of encouragement. If you want to learn more, visit his site. Go to: *http://pages.prodigy.net/mattgreen*

TODAY

I'll do what I can, with what I have, where I am.

"It's not easy being green."

Kermit the Frog

Do you feel different, alone, left out, or strange? Does it seem that how you look, act, think, and feel is unusual compared to everyone else? Are you considered an odd-ball or an outcast at school? Don't think of yourself as weird—think of yourself as *original*. You're an individual; you stand apart from the crowd. According to MTV political correspondent Tabitha Soren, "The ones who take a different path often end up being the innovators of society."

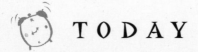

TODAY

I'm glad I'm an original.

"I always feel if you do right,
right will follow."

Oprah Winfrey

The world is full of wackos, bad news, tragedy, and grief…but it's also full of wonderful people, delightful surprises, goodness, and joy. You can choose to see the darkness, or you can focus on the light. The choice you make can shape your relationships, your achievements, and your life. Sometimes—despite all the evidence to the contrary—you simply have to *trust* that things will turn out okay. That if you reach out to someone, you'll make a friend. That if you do a kindness, it will come back to you. That right follows right.

 **TODAY**

I'll trust.

APRIL 11

"No matter how far you've gone
on a wrong road, turn back."

Turkish proverb

Angela had always been shy and reserved, but when she entered ninth grade, she was determined to stand out. She wanted everyone to think she was cool and tough, so she smoked, skipped class, and dressed all in black. At first, the other students seemed impressed with Angela's new image, and they waited to see what she would do next. But deep down, Angela felt trapped. She always had to think of new ways to attract attention, when what she really wanted was to have friends and to do well in school. She wished she could go back to being the "old" Angela.

TODAY

I won't be afraid to change course.

"Never doubt that a small group
of thoughtful, committed people can
change the world. Indeed it is
the only thing that ever has."

Margaret Mead

If there's a cause you care about deeply—hunger,
poverty, homelessness, abandoned pets, affordable
housing, racism, sexism, equal rights, land mines,
endangered species, pollution, the environment, or
whatever it is—find people who feel the way you do.
Then get started changing the world.

 **TODAY**

**I'll identify at least one thing I care
about deeply. Then I'll find at least one
person who feels the way I do.**

"What distinguishes us one from another
is our dreams…and what we do
to make them come about."

Joseph Epstein

Anisa Kintz, a student at Whittemore Park Middle School in Conway, South Carolina, dreams of a world where people of all races get along and respect each other. So she organized an annual Calling All Colors conference at Coastal Carolina University to promote racial unity among young people in grades 3–8. Similar conferences have since been held around the U.S., in Canada, and in New Zealand. Andrea was invited to speak on racial unity at a United Nations conference.

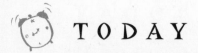 **TODAY**

**I'll work to make one
of my dreams come true.**

"Too much rest is rust."

Sir Walter Scott

Do you feel tired and rundown? Listless? Slow and dull, like a slug? Exercise can help. Working out releases *endorphins*—brain chemicals that make you feel energized and happier. So take a bike ride, dance around your room, go skateboarding, swim, or do yoga—whatever makes you feel good. (*Tip:* Regular exercise also makes you stronger and more fit.)

TODAY

I'll exercise.

"None of us is as smart as all of us."

Phil Condit

You've heard that two heads are better than one. And if two heads are better, why not three? Four? Or more? If you're struggling with a problem, facing a major decision, or coping with a serious issue in your life, you don't have to go it alone. And if you're in search of a fresh perspective, want to do some brainstorming, or are starting a new project, why not get input from other people you know?

**I'll ask other people for help,
advice, or ideas.**

> "Nobody can give you wiser advice
> than yourself."

Cicero

People will always give you advice (whether you want it or not). You'll probably hear "If I were you…" from your parents, other family members, teachers, classmates, and friends. Most of the time, advice givers have your best interests in mind, and their tips might be useful and helpful; you might even be grateful for them. But you should never act on advice that you doubt, even if it's from someone older (and supposedly wiser) than you. Do what *you* feel is right, what *you* think will bring the best results.

 **TODAY**

I'll take my own advice.

"Energy and persistence conquer all things."

Benjamin Franklin

What does it mean to persist? One definition says "to go on resolutely or stubbornly in spite of opposition." In other words, it means to keep going...and going...and going.... No matter what obstacles stand in your way, find the energy to keep reaching for your goals. (P.S. You've probably heard the old saying "If at first you don't succeed, try, try again," and maybe you yawn just thinking about it. The reason that old saying never dies is because it's *true*.)

TODAY

**I'll reconsider a goal
I've almost given up on.**

> "Our lives improve only when we
> take chances—and the first and
> most difficult risk we can take
> is to be honest with ourselves."
>
> *Walter Anderson*

Are you honest with yourself? Not just about your strengths and weaknesses, but also about the kind of person you are. Are you someone with strong values and beliefs? Can you say no to temptation and yes to opportunity? Do you know what you stand for and what you won't stand for? Are you true to yourself? You might consider these questions throughout the day. Write about them in your journal or talk about them with someone you trust.

 **TODAY**

I'll risk being honest with myself.

"Never bend your head. Hold it high.
Look the world straight in the eye."

Helen Keller

Your body language says a lot about you. When you're feeling good about yourself, you stand tall (vs. slouching), look people in the eye (rather than avoiding eye contact), and smile (instead of frowning or looking angry). In short, you appear more relaxed and confident. Even when you're feeling shy or uncertain, you can still practice positive body language. Hold your head high and look people in the eye, even if you feel uncomfortable at first. With practice, you'll get better and your confidence may increase.

 **TODAY**

I'll practice confident body language.

"Speak when you're angry, and you'll make
the best speech you'll ever regret."

Laurence J. Peter

Before you say those angry, hurtful words to someone
you care about…STOP. Put your hand over your mouth
if you have to. Then go somewhere else and try one or
more of these healthy ways to let your anger out:
- Hit a pillow.
- Hit the floor with a rolled-up magazine
  or newspaper.
- Go for a walk or a run.
- Shoot some baskets.
- Draw or paint an angry picture.
- Write in your journal.

Later, when you've calmed down, you can try talking to
the person—without making things worse.

 **TODAY**

**I'll stop myself before I say
something hurtful.**

"In order to go on living one must try to escape the death involved in perfection."

Hannah Arendt

Perfectionism is a trap. If you're afraid to take risks or make mistakes; if you're never satisfied with anything you do; if you set impossible or unrealistic goals for yourself; if you define your self-worth in terms of what you *do* instead of who you *are* as a person; if you're stressed out, anxious, and depressed much of the time…then you may be a perfectionist.

 **TODAY**

**I'll think about whether
I'm a perfectionist…and how
to ease up on myself.**

"The essence of being human is
that one does not seek perfection."

George Orwell

If you think you're a perfectionist, try these tips:

1. Get involved in activities that aren't rated, graded, or judged.

2. Change your self-talk. Eliminate "should," "I must," "I'd better," and "I have to."

3. Take a risk. Try something you've never done before. Don't worry about doing it perfectly.

4. Give yourself permission to make at least three mistakes a day…then go ahead and make them.

5. Join the human race. Perfection is boring! Our flaws, foibles, and imperfections make us unique and interesting.

 **TODAY**

I won't try to be perfect.

"You need chaos in your soul
to give birth to a dancing star."

Friedrich Nietzsche

When you're going through hard times—personal problems, doubts, worries, insecurities, fears—it's difficult to believe that anything good might result. Be patient. Talk with people you trust about your feelings. Ask for help solving problems you can't handle on your own. Write in your journal about what you're going through. The trouble you're having might lead to personal growth…or a burst of creativity. Hector Berlioz wrote his famous *Symphonie fantastique* when he was tormented by unrequited love.

 **TODAY**

**I'll know that hard times
can lead to good things.**

"We live in the present,
we dream of the future, but we learn
eternal truths from the past."

Madame Chiang Kai-shek

Think about your most embarrassing moment. (Maybe you were at your piano recital and couldn't play a note…or you lied to a teacher and got caught…or you wet your pants in first grade.) We all have moments we'd love to forget. It's human nature to make mistakes, goof up, and look ridiculous at times. We can't help it; mistakes are inevitable. So what can we do if we screw up? Forgive ourselves, let it go, and learn from it. As painful as they are, mistakes help us learn to be better people.

 **TODAY**

I'll learn from a mistake.

"If you have desire, determination and
work hard, you can achieve anything in life."

Chris Evert

What does it take to be a success? Good fortune? Lots
of money? A lucky break? Well, maybe…but success
also depends on hard work. And determination. And an
unwillingness to give up. Thomas Alva Edison, perhaps
the most famous inventor of all time, created more than
1,000 inventions—including the lightbulb. His success
didn't happen overnight. In fact, he tried 6,000 different
materials for his lightbulb before finding ones that
worked the way he wanted. Edison would have agreed
with this old saying: "Success comes before work only in
the dictionary."

 **T O D A Y**

**I'll work hard on something
I want to achieve.**

"How sweet to be a Cloud
Floating in the Blue!"

A.A. Milne, Winnie-the-Pooh

When was the last time you really relaxed? One of the best ways to let go of tension is with a deep breathing exercise. Here's how: Sit or lie still and close your eyes. Starting at your head, you'll relax all the muscles in your body by *tensing* them as you slowly inhale a deep breath, then *releasing* them as you slowly exhale. Begin with your neck and facial muscles; move down your body and end with your feet and toes. Count to five as you inhale and tense, five as you exhale and release. End with a final deep breath and imagine all of your stress flowing out of your body.

TODAY

I'll try a deep breathing exercise.

"Good timber does not grow with ease;
the stronger the wind,
the stronger the trees."

J. Willard Marriott

Challenges, problems, obstacles, hardships, hurts; depending on how you handle them, they all make you stronger. Nobody goes through life without experiencing suffering, sadness, and failure. Even the most successful people have struggled. Learn from them. Think of famous people you admire; visit the library and look for biographies, autobiographies, interviews, and profiles. If you find something that inspires you—a quote, story, or insight—you might want to write it in your journal.

 **TODAY**

I'll read about someone I admire.

"Obstacles don't have to stop you.
If you run into a wall, don't turn around
and give up. Figure out how to climb it,
go through it, or work around it."

Michael Jordan

It's fun to get advice from famous people. If there's someone you admire, you might write to him or her and ask questions like "What's the biggest challenge you have faced so far?" "What did you do?" "What did you learn?" "Do you have any words of wisdom to share?" Ask your librarian to help you find an address. Or check out *The Address Book* or *The Kid's Address Book* by Michael Levine; each includes thousands of addresses for famous people, and both are updated often. If you're lucky, you might get a response.

 **TODAY**

I'll write to someone I admire.

"Difficult times have helped me to understand better than before how infinitely rich and beautiful life is in every way and that so many things that one goes worrying about are of no importance whatsoever."

Isak Dinesen

Sometimes we spend the day complaining about little things—like being late, not getting called on in class, a messy room. Then we hear about something terrible that happened to someone else: an accident, a fire, a theft, an emergency, a disastrous loss. And suddenly all those things we were grumbling about seem awfully insignificant.

 **TODAY**

I'll keep things in perspective.

*"If you always do what interests you,
at least one person is pleased."*

Katharine Hepburn

You make many choices each day—what to eat, what to wear, and how to spend your free time. At school, you probably choose who to hang out with, which teams or clubs to join, and which elective classes to take. At home, you might decide whether to clean your room, spend time with your family, or do your homework. When you make choices, do you listen to your heart and decide what's best for you? Or do you opt for what might please your parents, friends, teachers, classmates, and the other people in your life? Pleasing *you* is important, too.

 **TODAY**

I'll make a choice that pleases me.

MAY 1

"I have a beautiful blank book and each night
before I go to bed, I write down five things
that I can be grateful about that day."

Sarah Ban Breathnach

Sarah Ban Breathnach calls this book her Gratitude
Journal, and for her, it has become a conscious way
to give thanks each day. When you write down your
blessings, large or small, you start noticing all the wonderful things in your life. You might write about a
compliment someone gave you, a meal your parents
cooked, a friend you love, or your pet. You might
explain why you're thankful for these things or just list
them—whatever works for you. Even (or especially) on
rough days, write down five things you're grateful for.
This will help you remember that some things are still
going well in your life.

 **TODAY**

I'll start a Gratitude Journal.

MAY 2

"I am only one, but still I am one. I cannot do everything, but still I can do something; and because I cannot do everything, I will not refuse to do something I can do."

Edward Everett Hale

Benilde-St. Margaret's High School in St. Louis Park, Minnesota, holds a special awards ceremony twice each year—always after school, so parents and grandparents can attend. The awards given out aren't the usual athletic or academic recognitions. Instead, students are "highly commended for achievement and dedication" to the school community. The honorees are teens who help out in the office or the computer lab, lend a hand in the classroom, exude good attitude, and generally make life easier and more pleasant for their teachers and peers.

 TODAY

I'll do what I can to help others.

✿ MAY 3 ✿

"If you approach the future pessimistically,
then you can be pretty certain the things you
fear most are going to happen."

Douglas Adams

You know you'll blow the test…and you do. You're
positive you won't finish your project on time…so you
don't. Are you living out fears that prevent you from
being your best? Try thinking positively for a change.
The next time you face a challenge, be optimistic. Look
forward to it. Welcome it. Greet it with a hopeful,
upbeat attitude. If this is too hard for you—if your fears
keep holding you back—get help. Talk with an adult
you trust.

 **TODAY**

I'll be optimistic.

✐ MAY 4 ✎

"People don't waste *hours*,
they waste *minutes*."

Jim Delisle

How much time do you waste just waiting? Waiting for a ride, waiting for someone to return a phone call, waiting for a Web site to load, waiting for a TV program to start, waiting for dinner, waiting, waiting…zzzzzzz. You don't have to do something every second of your life, but you probably waste more time than you know. Here's a sure cure for those squandered minutes (and hours): Always have something to read, and something to write with and on. Then you'll never be caught with nothing to do.

TODAY

I'll be conscious of the time I waste.

MAY 5

"A well-nourished body feels stronger and healthier, which can improve your whole outlook. Taking care of yourself—inside and out—is the key to higher self-esteem and greater self-confidence."

Tina Schwager and Michele Schuerger

What have you eaten today? Did you skip breakfast, grab a soft drink on the way out the door, eat fast food for lunch, and munch on a fistful of cookies before dinner? Or maybe you've nibbled on nothing but celery because you're on a diet. Either way, you're abusing your body. It needs nourishing foods (containing vitamins, minerals, proteins, and carbohydrates) for optimum performance. This means eating a *balanced* diet including lots of fruits and veggies; breads, cereals, and pastas; dairy products; and meat or alternative sources of protein. When you *eat* well, you *feel* well.

 **TODAY**

I'll eat a balanced diet.

MAY 6

> "Food is an important part
> of a balanced diet."
>
> *Fran Lebowitz*

Food is our fuel—it's our body's main source of energy, vitamins, and minerals. Are you eating enough to keep your body healthy and strong? To build a better body inside and out, start with good nutrition. Say no to: (1) *diets* (read more about why they don't work on page 19), (2) *too much junk food* (limit the salty chips and sugary treats), and (3) *skipping meals* (start with a good breakfast, eat lunch and dinner, don't forget your fruits and veggies, and snack between meals). If you're not eating well, or if you're barely eating at all, ask yourself if something's bothering you. This may be a sign of a deeper problem.

 **TODAY**

I'll build a healthy body.

"I think stress, anxiety, and pressure
from society have a lot to do
with eating disorders."

Susan, age 14

For some people, eating is a daily battle. Do you know someone who has an eating disorder, or are you suffering from one yourself? People with eating disorders either starve themselves (*anorexia*), binge eat and purge their food (*bulimia*), or eat uncontrollably (*compulsive overeating disorder*). All of these life-threatening illnesses are on the rise among young people today. The good news is: *Help is available.* To learn more, visit the National Eating Disorders Association online at *www.nationaleatingdisorders.org* or call 1-800-931-2237 for information and support. (P.S. It's a myth that boys don't get eating disorders—they do.)

 **TODAY**

I'll ask myself if I have
a problem with eating.

MAY 8

"If there are adults you admire, don't be afraid
to ask them for help and advice."

Earvin "Magic" Johnson

Every young person needs at least one safe adult in his
or her life—someone who can offer information and
support. Perhaps a parent plays this role in your life; if
not, you need another safe adult. A relative, teacher,
school counselor, coach, youth leader, or clergy member
can fill this need. If you think you might have an eating
disorder or another serious problem, *you need to get
help.* Talk to your safe adult. Don't keep the problem a
secret anymore.

 **TODAY**

I'll find a safe adult to talk to.

MAY · 9

"Opportunity is missed by most people
because it is dressed in overalls
and looks like work."

Thomas Alva Edison

Ami beamed with pride as the tennis coach handed her the Most Valuable Player Award for the third year in a row. Colleen, one of her teammates, whispered to another player, "She's so lucky. They pick her every year." Colleen didn't realize that luck had little to do with it: Ami never missed tennis practice, she spent her Saturday mornings volleying balls with her dad, and she babysat to earn money to pay for her own tennis lessons. She worked harder than anyone else on the team, and it showed.

 **TODAY**

**I'll look for a new opportunity,
even if it means work.**

✿ MAY 10 ✿

"Call it a clan, call it a network,
call it a tribe, call it family. Whatever you
call it, whoever you are, you need one."

Jane Howard

Here's an Aesop's fable you might have heard: An old man was dying, so he gathered his sons around him to give them some parting advice. He ordered his servants to bring in a bundle of sticks, then said to his eldest son "Break it." The son tried but couldn't break the bundle. The other sons tried and also failed. Then the father said "Untie the bundle and each of you take a stick. Then break the stick." The sticks broke easily. The moral of the fable: There's strength in unity.

 **TODAY**

I'll be glad I have a family.

MAY 11

"It is not because things are difficult
that we do not dare. It is because we
do not dare that they are difficult."

Seneca

Think of something you've wanted to do for a long time. It might be anything…asking someone out, talking to a friend about a problem you're having, taking on a new challenge, speaking out about something important to you. Why haven't you done it yet? Does it seem too hard? Too scary? It might be that your fears are making it seem more difficult than it really is. In the words of author, businessman, and motivational speaker Earl Nightingale, "Courage changes things for the better." Gather your courage and give it a try.

 **TODAY**

I'll be daring.

✿ MAY 12 ✿

"You can't shake hands with a closed fist."

Indira Gandhi

People have different opinions, beliefs, and points of view, so it's normal and natural for conflicts to arise. (Some conflict is even healthy.) But physical force—whether with fists, feet, or weapons—is not the answer. You may win the fight, but if your goal is to resolve the conflict, you'll lose. If you're too mad to talk, walk away. If you want to try talking, take a deep breath, count to 10 (or higher), then speak more slowly and softly than usual. And be sure to *listen* when the other person speaks.

 **TODAY**

I'll try to resolve a conflict without fighting or shouting.

MAY 13

"I didn't *lose* the gold. I *won* the silver."

Michelle Kwan

Following the 1998 Winter Olympics in Nagano, Japan, Michelle Kwan was besieged by reporters asking "You lost the gold—how does that feel?" News broadcasts about the competition described Michelle as "settling" for silver and coming in a "disappointing second." True, she was predicted to win the gold medal for women's figure skating. But Michelle doesn't agree that if you're not #1, you're a loser. When she appeared on the *Tonight* show with Jay Leno soon after winning her silver medal—mature, articulate, proud of her accomplishments—Jay called her "a true American hero."

TODAY

**I don't have to be the best
to be a winner.**

✿ MAY 14 ✿

"What lies behind us and what lies
before us are small matters compared to
what lies within us."

Ralph Waldo Emerson

Yesterday and all the days before are gone; tomorrow is still to come. You have this moment—here and now—to relish and cherish your talents, capabilities, skills, and gifts. Make the most of today. Be the best you can be. In the words of Deepak Chopra, "The past is history, the future is a mystery, and this moment is a gift. That is why this moment is called the *present*."

 **TODAY**

I'll cherish who and what I am.

✐ MAY 15 ✐

"Be kind, for everyone you meet is
fighting a harder battle."

Plato

There's no way to know what's really happening in
someone else's life. The most popular, attractive, and
successful person at school might have problems you're
clueless about. Even on bad days, you can spread a little
kindness—a smile, a gesture, a word, a generous and
unexpected act. You might brighten another person's
day, and you'll feel better about yourself.

 **TODAY**

I'll be kind.

MAY 16

"Your mind is like a tipi. Leave the entrance
flap open so that the fresh air can enter
and clear out the smoke of confusion."

Chief Eagle, Teton Sioux

Is your mind open to new ideas, new experiences,
new people? Or have you already decided that there are
ideas you're not interested in, experiences you don't
want to have, and people you don't want to know?
Here's a short list of things that can keep your mind
closed: Fear. Prejudice. Habit. Hatred. Ignorance.
Suspicion. And sometimes, sheer laziness. When you
have an open mind, you can get answers to questions
that are bothering you. You can learn new things. You
can grow and change.

 **TODAY**

I'll be more open-minded.

✿ MAY 17 ✿

"Great works are performed
not by strength but by perseverance."

Samuel Johnson

I think I can, I think I can, I think I can…. You probably know the classic children's story about the little engine that was determined to pull a huge, heavy load up a mountain. *Slow and steady wins the race….* And you might have heard the fable of the tortoise and the hare, in which a tortoise bests a speedy hare by taking measured, purposeful steps and refusing to give up. For fun, you could ask a children's librarian to point you toward other old favorites with similar messages: You don't have to be the strongest or the fastest to succeed.

TODAY

**I'll take one step toward finishing
a big project I'm working on.**

✿ MAY 18 ✿

"Never put off enjoyment
because there's no time like the pleasant."

Evan Esar

Don't put off being happy until your life has the right set of conditions ("Once I'm out of high school…" "The day my grades start going up…" "When I get a job…" "When I have a boyfriend/girlfriend…"). Instead, be happy now. Wake up thankful for each new day; go to bed satisfied with your life and all you have. You can make happiness a habit. *Tip:* If you're truly unhappy right now and you can't seem to shake your feelings of sadness or anger, talk to an adult you trust. A parent, teacher, school counselor, or clergy member may be able to help.

 **TODAY**

**I'll make a list of things
I'm happy about.**

"No matter what language we speak,
we all live under the same moon and stars."

John Denver

So many things divide us: language barriers, boundaries on the map, politics, different customs and beliefs. But in many ways, people are the same all over the world. We all laugh and cry, we live and die. We share the same planet and breathe the same air. Perhaps we're more connected than we know.

 **TODAY**

**I'll look for ways people
are more alike than different.**

"To solve the problems of today,
we must focus on tomorrow."

Erik Nupponen

Every problem you face has a potential solution—or several. But before you choose the easiest one, or the one that seems best, think it through. Try to predict the consequences. Weigh the possible outcomes. Picture various scenarios in your mind: "If I tell Alonzo I don't like the way he's treating me, he might get angry. But if I don't tell him, he'll keep treating me that way." If you're stuck between a rock and a hard place, talk with a wise friend or adult. Get his or her input into what you might do.

TODAY

**I'll predict the consequences
of a choice I'm considering.**

"A musician must make music, an artist must paint, a poet must write, if he is to be ultimately at peace with himself. What one can be, one must be."

Abraham Maslow

What do you feel the urge to do? When you lie awake at night and dream, or gaze out the window during school, what do you see yourself doing? Making music? Painting? Writing? Skydiving? Climbing mountains? Doing stand-up comedy in a crowded club? Designing a building? Creating a stained-glass window? Raising horses? Racing cars? Don't fight it! Learn more about your passion. Talk to people who live your dream. Gather information and find out how you can get there.

 **TODAY**

I'll start being what I must be.

✿ MAY 22 ✿

"A celebrity is a person who is
known for his well-knownness."

Daniel Boorstin

Quick: Name your top three role models. Are they people you know personally—a parent, a teacher, a friend? Or are they celebrities? It's easy to pick actors, athletes, rock stars, rappers, talk show hosts, super-models, etc. as role models. You see them almost everywhere—in the movies, on TV, in advertisements, in magazines—and they seem so perfect. But before you choose celebrities as your role models, learn more about them. Have they done anything commendable? Do they deserve your admiration?

 **TODAY**

**I'll think about my role models—
and whether they're worth looking up to.**

"I'm sure I'll get where I want to go.
My parents taught us to believe in
ourselves, to have confidence."

Venus Williams

Many athletes use *visualization*—mental imagery—to boost their confidence and envision their success. This means mentally rehearsing their performance, step by step, and imagining themselves scoring the goal, winning the race, or achieving their personal best. You can use visualization to help you succeed. Start with a relaxation exercise (see pages 78, 79, and 117 for examples). Once you're feeling calm and centered, close your eyes and imagine yourself facing a challenge. Visualize in vivid detail each step you'll take, then imagine yourself succeeding. You can use this technique anytime, anywhere.

TODAY

I'll practice visualization.

> "You miss 100 percent of the shots
> you never take."

Wayne Gretzky

The world's best quarterbacks complete only 60 percent of their passes. The greatest basketball stars make only 50 percent of their shots. And most major league baseball players get on base just 25 percent of the time. But that doesn't stop them from taking their shot at glory. Is something stopping you?

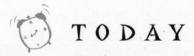 **TODAY**

I'll take one risk.

"The courage to be is the courage to accept oneself, in spite of being unacceptable."

Paul Tillich

Artists and other creative types are famously eccentric. In 1993, rock star Prince changed his name to an unpronounceable symbol. J.D. Salinger, author of *The Catcher in the Rye*, is a recluse who has refused to publish anything since 1965. He still writes, but he locks his work in a safe and won't let anyone see it. If you're creative, chances are you're a bit...unusual. You're not alone!

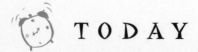

TODAY

I'll enjoy my creativity.

MAY 26

"Freedom is nothing else
but a chance to be better."

Albert Camus

Andy's parents go out of town for the weekend, leaving him alone in the house. FREEDOM! He calls his friends, they come over to party, they call more friends, and before long the house is trashed and the police are out front. That's not freedom. That's a dumb stunt that guarantees Andy's parents won't trust him again. Real freedom brings responsibility; the choices you make are up to you, and so are the consequences. Many teens equate freedom with drinking and other drug use, sexual activity, and other risky behaviors that can mess up their lives. They misuse their freedom and end up trapped.

 **TODAY**

I'll use my freedom responsibly.

MAY 27

"The more I want to get something done,
the less I call it work."

Richard Bach

Some people drag themselves to work every morning; other people can't wait to get there. The difference is having a job you enjoy. It's not too soon to start thinking about your future. What would you like to do? What can you picture yourself doing? Even if you get a part-time job now, you can try to find one in an organization or business that means something to you. Talk with adults who love their jobs; ask their advice.

 **TODAY**

I'll picture myself in a job I enjoy.

MAY 28

"They're like my best friends, only bester."

Zac Hanson

Heartthrob Zac Hanson was talking about his older brothers, Isaac and Taylor, when he said this. They don't just "MMMbop" together; they actually *like* each other. Do you feel the same way about your siblings (if you have them)? What makes some siblings the best of friends, while others seem to be rivals or even enemies most of the time? Can you think of ways you might become a better sibling?

 **TODAY**

I'll be a better brother or sister.

MAY 29

"One act of real usefulness is worth
all the abstract sentiment in the world."

Ann Radcliff

You read about starving children and feel sorry for them. You hear of a family whose home was destroyed by fire and feel sad. You see a news report about a flood, hurricane, or earthquake and feel compassion for the thousands of people who have been hurt or left homeless. It's good that these problems touch your emotions, but feeling isn't enough. What can you do? How can you help? Who can you call to learn more? Who might join you in trying to make a difference?

 **TODAY**

**I'll do something specific
to help someone in need.**

"I never intended to become
a run-of-the-mill person."

Barbara Jordan

Barbara Jordan was the first black student at Boston University Law School; from 1966–1972, she was the only woman and the only black person in the Texas Senate; from 1973–1979, she was a member of the U.S. House of Representatives. Her numerous awards included induction into the National Women's Hall of Fame and the African-American Hall of Fame. She was an achiever because she worked hard—and because she never intended to be anything else.

 **TODAY**

I'll set my sights high.

"Today is the first day
of the rest of your life."

Abbie Hoffman

Seize this day—make it yours, starting now. Love
the Earth, the animals, yourself, and others. Drink in
the sun and fresh air. Be kind and giving. Learn. Ask
questions. Find answers. Satisfy your curiosity. Be
thankful for this day. Live it with a thirst. (P.S. Want to
impress your friends? Say *carpe diem*, which is Latin for
"seize the day.")

 **TODAY**

I'll seize the day.

≜ JUNE 1 ≜

"I wonder what it would be like to live
in a world where it was always June."

Lucy Maud Montgomery

Ahhhh…it's June at last. School's out, summer's here, and it's time for rest and relaxation. You have three delicious months of free time stretching out before you. What are your plans? Are you going on vacation, to camp, or any other special place? Do you have an idea for a new project, hobby, or collection? How will you make the most of the lazy days of summer? Almost any adult you know would gladly trade places with you. As author Henry James once wrote, "Summer afternoon— summer afternoon; to me those have always been the two most beautiful words in the English language."

 **TODAY**

I'll start planning my summer.

≜ JUNE 2 ≜

"I don't think you're much good,
unless you're doing good to someone."

Rose Kennedy

Imagine that right now, this moment, you had to give an accounting of your life so far—based solely on how much good you've done for others. How would you score? Rank yourself from 1 to 10, with 1 being the lowest score and 10 being the highest. If you scored high, congratulations and keep it up! If you scored low, make it a personal goal to start doing good, then follow through. You'll feel terrific about yourself. (For a list of other benefits, see pages 272–273.)

 **TODAY**

I'll do good.

"An undefined problem has
an infinite number of solutions."

Robert A. Humphrey

Before you can solve a problem, you need to know what the problem really is. You need to define it as clearly as you can. Think it through. Consider it from all sides. Write it down using simple words. And try not to bring in a lot of extraneous stuff—other problems that aren't related to the one you're trying to solve, irrelevant details, past hurts and misunderstandings. Once you define a problem, you can focus on solutions specific to that problem without getting sidetracked or confused.

 **TODAY**

**I'll define a problem
that's been bothering me.**

≜ JUNE 4 ≜

"We can't take any credit for our talents.
It's how we use them that counts."

Madeleine L'Engle

Maybe you were born with a beautiful singing voice, or the grace of a dancer, or a talent for sculpting. Unless you use your voice, your muscles, or your hands, you'll never know how far your talent can take you. So sing, dance, or create art. Train, practice, and work hard. Make the most of your gifts.

 **TODAY**

I'll use my talent(s).

≜ JUNE 5 ≜

"The more I do, the more I can do."

Christopher Reeve

He was a movie star (*Superman*) when a horse riding accident made him a quadriplegic. Today Christopher Reeve is a spokesman for people with disabilities. He can't move on his own, so he uses a motorized wheelchair, which he operates by blowing or sipping on a straw. He has started a foundation, lobbied Congress, spoken out at the Democratic National Convention, written a book (*Still Me*), and traveled the country making speeches. "Sitting around doing nothing and sleeping do not agree with me," he says.

 **TODAY**

I won't sit around doing nothing.

⛰ JUNE 6 ⛰

> "It's not enough to have a good mind.
> The main thing is to use it well."
>
> *René Descartes*

Andy was bright, but his school performance didn't show it. His teachers often said that he could do well if he "applied himself," which he chose not to do. During the summer before tenth grade, Andy enrolled in a story writing class at his local community center. He discovered that he loved creating characters, writing dialogue, and sharing his stories with the group. One day he realized that the subjects he took in school—history, grammar, literature, and others—could help him write better stories. By the end of the summer, he was actually looking forward to school.

 **TODAY**

I'll sign up for a summer class.

"There are billions of people in the world,
and every one of them is special.
No one else in the world is like you."

Muhammad Ali

You may have your mom's eyes, your dad's feet, and
your Aunt Martha's talent for playing the bassoon, but
you're completely unique. No one else on earth is
exactly like you. Take a moment to list 10 things about
you that are special. Write anything, serious or silly; you
don't have to show your list to anyone. If you can't think
of anything to write, ask a trusted friend to help you
come up with ideas.

 **TODAY**

I'll think about how special I am.

▲ JUNE 8 ▲

"There is no pillow so soft
as a clear conscience."

French proverb

You did something wrong; do you hide it or admit it? Most of us want to conceal our mistakes or wrongs. We feel ashamed and worry about the consequences of our actions. So we lie or deny, but in our hearts we know the truth. A guilty conscience can keep you up all night, tossing and turning until morning. So admit what you did. Ask for forgiveness. Do what you can to make it right…and rest easy tonight.

 TODAY

I'll admit a wrong and make it right.

"I will persist until I succeed. Always will
I take another step. If that is of no avail
I will take another, and yet another. In truth,
one step at a time is not too difficult....
I know that small attempts, repeated,
will complete any undertaking."

Og Mandino

One step at a time. Small attempts, repeated. Keep these words in mind no matter what you attempt, and you'll reach any goal you set for yourself. If a single step seems too big or daunting, you can always break it up into smaller steps. If a particular goal seems too hard to reach, you can always break it up into a series of smaller goals.

 **TODAY**

**I'll take one step toward
a goal that's important to me.**

≜ JUNE 10 ≜

"Animals are such agreeable friends—they ask
no questions, they pass no criticisms."

George Eliot

If you have a pet, you already know that an animal can
be a wonderful, loyal friend. But do you also know that
many experts believe spending time with an animal can
lower your stress level and make you happier and
healthier? Next time you're feeling anxious or upset, pet
your cat, walk your dog, or watch your fish swimming
around. If you don't have any pets, visit a friend who
does or volunteer at your local animal shelter.

 **TODAY**

I'll spend time with an animal friend.

⩕ JUNE 11 ⩕

"My whole life is an adventure.
But you don't have to do something racy
and wild to have an adventure. You can
have one in your own backyard."

Gary Paulsen

You don't have to wait until you're grown to have an adventurous life. You don't have to be big, strong, daring, or wealthy to be an adventurer. It's a matter of attitude and perspective—with creativity, imagination, and inventiveness thrown in. An adventure doesn't have to mean jumping out of an airplane, sailing around the world, or going on safari. It can be a journey of self-discovery, a quest, an achievement, a positive risk, an event, a project that excites you…whatever you want, large scale or small.

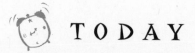 **TODAY**

I'll plan a summer adventure.

≜ JUNE 12 ≜

> "Each blade of grass has its Angel that bends
> over it and whispers, 'Grow, grow.'"
>
> *The Talmud*

Do you have a backyard garden, a windowbox full
of flowers, or some potted houseplants that you care
for? Tending a garden or nurturing plants indoors is a
wonderful way to feel connected to nature and to practice caring for living things. Talk to your family about
planting a backyard flower garden together or growing
vegetables and herbs. If you live in an apartment, you
might consider starting a container garden on your
patio or windowsill. If you live in a city, find out if
there's a local urban gardening program so you can
grow vegetables or herbs in a community plot.

 **TODAY**

I'll consider planting a garden.

☖ JUNE 13 ☖

"In my music, I'm trying to play the truth
of what I am. The reason it's difficult is
because I'm changing all the time."

Charles Mingus

Charles Mingus was one of the most gifted and important jazz artists of all time. (You might try listening to some of his music; start with *Blues and Roots* or *Mingus Ah Um*, or ask a jazz buff for recommendations.) He was constantly seeking, experimenting—and changing, which is one reason why his music is so exciting. You're changing, too, as you learn and grow, and that's part of what makes life so exciting. Consider how you've changed within the past month, six months, or year. Which changes have been positive? Which haven't?

TODAY

I'll think about how I've changed.

⟁ JUNE 14 ⟁

> "If you want happiness for a lifetime,
> help someone else."
>
> *Chinese proverb*

Each and every week, high school senior Josh Root gets together with a 12-year-old named Joe for roller-skating, swimming, and trips to the arcade. It's part of a service project organized by his congregation, Mt. Olivet Lutheran in Minneapolis, Minnesota. Josh knows that his volunteer work helps the community, but he also admits to doing it "for very selfish reasons. I help you, you help me—it just gives me a feel-good euphoria."

TODAY

I'll help someone else.

⚞ JUNE 15 ⚟

"The future has a way
of arriving unannounced."

George F. Will

Time goes faster as you get older. If you haven't felt this yet, ask an adult. Before you know it, you'll be out of high school, past college, all grown up and (maybe) with kids of your own. You can't slow time, but you can prevent it from sneaking up on you. One way to do this is by keeping a daily journal. Recording your thoughts, accomplishments, goals, and experiences gives you a sense of control over your life. And when the future arrives, you'll have a past to look back on—in writing.

 **TODAY**

If I don't already keep a journal, I'll start one.

"Tomorrow hopes we have learned
something from yesterday."

John Wayne

Each new day gives us a chance to correct a mistake,
right a wrong, solve a problem, or mend a relationship.
What did you learn today that you didn't know yesterday? What can you do today to have a better tomorrow?

 **TODAY**

**I'll remember what yesterday taught me,
and I'll use that knowledge today.**

≜ JUNE 17 ≜

"When a deep injury is done us,
we never recover until we forgive."

Alan Paton

When someone hurts us, we may hold onto feelings of hatred and resentment. We may wish the person harm or even plot revenge. This consumes our time, eats up our energy, and keeps the hurt from healing. Dwelling on what happened, turning it over and over in our minds, and imagining how we'll retaliate makes it difficult to move on with our lives. First we must find a way to forgive.

TODAY

**I'll forgive an old injury
so I can put it behind me.**

"Acceptance is not submission;
it is acknowledgment of the facts
of the situation. Then deciding what
you're going to do about it."

Kathleen Casey Theisen

Some problems simply aren't solvable. Maybe the circumstances are beyond your control; maybe the solution isn't up to you alone, and the other person isn't willing or able to do his or her part. Admitting when a problem is beyond you isn't the same as running away from it. Instead, it's being realistic about what you can and can't do.

 **TODAY**

**I'll accept that some problems
aren't solvable.**

"You have to go through difficulties
to open up and understand life.
If you're always in a sugary,
round place, you never go anywhere."

Juliette Binoche

Your parents may try to keep you safe. They'll shield
you from certain types of information, people, and
experiences. That's a good thing—up to a point. If you
feel that your parents are overprotective, negotiate for
more freedom. Set up a meeting and talk about
it. Explain what you need from them; ask what they
need from you. See if you can reach common ground.
Tip: Most parents are willing to loosen the reigns a little
when kids are trustworthy, honest, and responsible.

 **TODAY**

**If I think I need more freedom,
I'll talk with my parents.**

"We can try to avoid making choices
by doing nothing, but even that is a decision."

Gary Collins

Hmmmm…Do *this* or do *that?* Which is the best choice? No one can know for sure, which is why decision making seems so scary. You can agonize over your choices forever, but this won't lead you anywhere. In the words of humorist Will Rogers, "Even if you're on the right track, you'll get run over if you just sit there."

TODAY

I'll make a decision.

≜ JUNE 21 ≜

"Hold a true friend with both your hands."

Nigerian proverb

Sometimes we take our friendships for granted. We break plans or forget to call. We go on and on about our own problems, ignoring or overlooking the fact that our friends might have troubles, too. True friends will forgive us these faults and be understanding…which is just one of many reasons to cherish our true friends.

TODAY

**I'll tell or show a friend
how much I care.**

"I don't ever want to be a man. I want always to be a little boy and to have fun."

James Barrie, Peter Pan

Would you like to stay young forever, like Peter Pan? Some people wish they could. Author Madeleine L'Engle once received a letter from a girl who asked "How can I stay a child forever and never grow up?" The author wrote back and said "You can't, and it wouldn't be a good idea if you could. But what you can do, and what I hope you will do, is stay a child forever *and* grow up." How can you find a way to do both? *Tip:* Ask your parents or grandparents what they liked best about you when you were younger. According to them, what were your best qualities? Do you still have some of those qualities? Why or why not?

 TODAY

I'll remember a favorite place, event, or toy from my childhood.

> "It takes a lot of makeup to make
> me look like the kind of woman
> who doesn't wear makeup."

Salma Hayek

Have you ever tried to look like someone you're not? Maybe there's a group you'd love to be in, so you copy their clothes and hairstyles. Or maybe you know someone who's a total poser. Beneath those cool clothes, radical hair, piercings, and tattoos is the kid you used to ride bikes with in fourth grade. It's normal to want to change your appearance, and trying different looks can be fun. But the kind of person you are should show through, no matter what you wear.

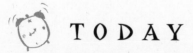

TODAY

I won't hide the real me.

"There is no place in the world where courtesy is so necessary as in the home."

Helen Hathaway

For some reason, many people think that home is the place where they can let it all hang out. They're rude, crude, obnoxious, and thoughtless. (They call it "just being themselves.") But if manners make life more pleasant for everyone—which they do—doesn't it make sense to be *especially* polite at home, where you spend so much of your time and where people (supposedly) care most about each other? Try it and see what happens. *Tip:* This might be a good topic for a family meeting. See page 58 for pointers.

TODAY

I'll use good manners at home.

≜ JUNE 25 ≜

"How much more grievous are
the consequences of anger
than the causes of it."

Marcus Aurelius

Have you ever gotten angry and taken it out on someone you love? Maybe you yelled at your mom or dad,
picked on your sister, hit your brother, or kicked the
dog. Even if they weren't the cause of your anger—and
even if they were trying to help—you used them as
targets simply because they were there. Find other ways
to vent your anger. Try brainstorming a list to have on
hand for the next time you lose your temper. *Tip:* This
might be a good topic for a family meeting. See page 58.

 **TODAY**

**If I get angry, I won't take it out
on someone I love.**

≜ JUNE 26 ≜

"Being able to laugh got me through."

Toni Morrison

She's written some of the most important novels of our time (or any time)—*Song of Solomon, Beloved, Paradise,* and others. But Toni Morrison's life hasn't always been easy. "There were plenty of roadblocks along the way," she remembers. "The world back then didn't expect much from a little black girl." In 1993, she was awarded the Nobel Prize for Literature, one of the world's most prestigious honors. And she's still laughing.

 **TODAY**

I'll keep laughing.

"Drawing is my passion. I would have done it whether I made money or not."

Mary Engelbreit

What's your favorite thing to do? Sing, write stories, build model rockets, dance, paint, solve math problems, collect rocks, take care of animals? Is there an activity that interests you so much that you lose track of time when you're doing it? What makes you feel positive, happy, and utterly content? If you've found that activity, make time for it. Don't let it slip away. If you haven't yet found it, start looking. Try new things until you discover what really interests you.

 **TODAY**

I'll do my favorite thing.

"I live in a community where many rock stars
live or visit. Hands down, all of them tell me
their teenage years were miserable.
Most of them are yesterday's losers."

M.E. Kerr

Relatively few adults look back on their teenage years
as the best years of their lives. (You might survey your
parents and neighbors on this issue.) Adolescence is a
time of changes and challenges, of fitting in (or not)
and finding out who you are. On some days you'll think
you're the most miserable person on the planet; on
other days you'll be on top of the world. As you ride
these highs and lows (and hang on for dear life), it helps
to remember that you're not the only person on the
roller coaster.

 **TODAY**

**I know I'm not alone.
I have people I can talk to.**

"My goal is simple. It is complete
understanding of the universe,
why it is as it is and why it exists at all."

Stephen Hawking

What would you like to understand? To know more
about? To explore? World-renowned theoretical physi-
cist Stephen Hawking has set his sights high...and
so can you. Or you might pursue a different type of
understanding. Many successful people have built their
careers around passionate curiosities and questions.
Think of something (anything) you'd like to understand, then brainstorm ways to start getting answers.
Who knows; this simple exercise might lead you to your
life's work.

 **TODAY**

**I'll name at least one thing
I want to understand.**

"Laziness may appear attractive,
but work gives satisfaction."

Anne Frank

Who wants to do chores during the summertime?
Nobody! So you ignore the dirty clothes in your room,
put off mowing the lawn, pretend the house doesn't
need to be vacuumed, forget to wash the dishes, and
neglect to take out the trash. You're having fun, taking
summer classes, hanging out with your friends, watching TV, surfing the Internet, or…what's your excuse?
Who will do your chores if you don't? *Tip:* Just do
them—without grumbling, whining, or complaining.
No more procrastinating. No new excuses. Focus on
how you'll feel when you're done: relieved, satisfied,
proud of yourself.

TODAY

I'll get busy.

☀ JULY 1 ☀

"One of these days is none of these days."

H.G. Bohn

Are you an "I'll do it tomorrow" kind of person? Have you been putting off something you'd really like to try? Do you tell yourself that now's not the time, you don't have the time, or you'll get around to it...one of these days?

TODAY

I'll do something
I've been meaning to do.

✦ JULY 2 ✦

"Life isn't about finding yourself.
Life is about creating yourself."

George Bernard Shaw

Trying to "find yourself" is like searching for the sunglasses that are perched on top of your head. They were never lost in the first place, and neither are you! Think of yourself in terms of raw materials: body, brain, ears, mouth, eyes, strength, skills, potential. Imagine that you're an artist, working with those materials to create something entirely new and wonderful—a painting, a sculpture, perhaps a collage. Now see the final product in your mind. What kind of self can you create?

 **TODAY**

I'll take a step toward creating myself.

"We ourselves feel that what we are
doing is just a drop in the ocean.
But the ocean would be less
because of that missing drop."

Mother Teresa

No one else on earth thinks just like you, has dreams like yours, or has precisely the same gifts and abilities. No matter who you are or what you become, you'll leave your unique imprint on the world. In the words of Mary Kay Blakely: "One life stamps and influences another, which in turn stamps and influences another, on and on, until the soul of human experience breathes on in generations we'll never even meet."

 **TODAY**

I'll be a positive influence.

☆ JULY 4 ☆

*"Character is much easier
kept than recovered."*

Thomas Paine

Life is full of temptations—to cheat, steal, lie, use alcohol or other drugs, have sex too soon, and take other dangerous risks. Don't compromise your character. If someone is trying to convince you to act in a way that might hurt you, resist—and get help if you need it. Talk to a friend you respect or a caring adult you trust. If your character needs repairs, it won't be easy, but it won't get easier if you wait until tomorrow. Decide what kind of person you want to be, then make that your goal.

TODAY

I won't compromise my character.

"Our life is frittered away by detail....
Simplify, simplify."

Henry David Thoreau

Do you have too much stuff? Old clothes cluttering your drawers and closet, toys and books you've grown out of, things you no longer use? Summertime is a great time to take stock of what you still want and need…and get rid of the rest. Homeless shelters, day care centers, charitable organizations, "free stores," and more will gladly take your castoffs if they're clean and in good condition. Find out where you can donate, then do it. You might make this a family project, or check with your neighbors to see if they want to participate.

 **TODAY**

I'll simplify my life.

"I try to live by the belief that you should always be yourself and do the things that are right for you. That means being realistic about your goals."

Tiger Woods

When other people advise you to "be realistic," what they usually mean is "You're aiming too high" or "Don't set yourself up for disappointment" or "That's impossible." They may mean well, but why let their perceptions limit you? You know your skills, talents, and abilities; you know what you're capable of doing. Decide what's realistic for you, then pursue it.

TODAY

I'll be realistic about my goals.

"Turn your face to the sun,
and the shadows fall behind you."

Maori proverb

You have thousands of thoughts each day, some positive and some negative. Do you let your negative thoughts crowd out the positive ones? Negative thoughts are like those huge cartoon snowballs that roll down a hill, growing larger and larger until they squash the unfortunate character standing below. You think a negative thought ("Alan doesn't like me"), which leads to another one ("Nobody likes me"), and then another—and soon you're convinced that your life stinks. When this starts to happen, tell yourself you're snowballing, then make yourself think a positive thought. Let the positive thought melt away your negative thought, like the sun melts the snow.

 **TODAY**

**I'll think a positive thought
to melt away a negative one.**

❋ JULY 8 ❋

"If you're not marching to your own tune,
you're going to be marching to someone else's.
You have to take control of your own life,
set your own priorities, or someone will be
happy to set them for you."

Elizabeth Dole

Whose tune are you marching to? Parents, teachers, and other adults have expectations for you, and that's not all bad. Friends may want you to act, think, or dress in certain ways. But there will come a time when you'll have to take charge of your own life, and you might as well start now. You can begin by figuring out your priorities. What's important to you? What do you care most about? What would you like to do with your life? (Can you hear the first notes of your own tune?)

 **TODAY**

I'll make a list of my priorities.

"The talent for being happy is
appreciating and liking what you have,
instead of what you don't have."

Woody Allen

Do you know someone who's always saying "If only I
had a better body, new clothes, different looks, nicer
hair" (or whatever), "then I'd really be happy"? (Or
maybe that someone is you?) Many people fall into the
trap of believing their happiness depends on their
appearance. Real happiness is based not on your *look*
but your *outlook*. Instead of focusing on what you
lack (or think you lack), try appreciating your positive
qualities. You'll feel better about how you look and who
you are.

 **TODAY**

I'll focus on my good qualities.

> "Never let anyone stop you
> from doing something that you
> believe in your heart you can do."

Jackie Joyner-Kersee

Winner of three gold, one silver, and three bronze Olympic medals, four world titles, and three Goodwill Games titles, Jackie Joyner-Kersee is considered the world's greatest female athlete. She holds world records in the heptathlon and the long jump and has racked up a multitude of awards. Her road to success wasn't easy; she grew up in poverty, battled asthma, coped with hostility toward girls' athletics, and survived her father's bullying and her mother's death. Today she's an inspiration and a role model to millions.

 **TODAY**

I'll follow my heart.

☀ JULY 11 ☀

"Procrastination—I'll deal with it
sooner or later."

Bumper sticker

Procrastination (otherwise known as the art of denial)
makes it hard to get anything done. If there's something
you've been procrastinating about, try a technique
recommended by Robert D. Rutherford: "David-and-
Goliath it." See yourself battling a big, annoying, stub-
born giant. Face the giant squarely and knock him
down. Savor your victory and reward yourself.

TODAY

I'll deal with it now.

✷ JULY 12 ✷

"Even though we're all just a small part
of the big picture, we can make a difference.
All of our actions—no matter how small—
have a rippling effect on the universe."

Madonna

When you think about making a difference, you might tell yourself "I'm just one person! What can I possibly do?" Start small, if you want: Recycle your soda cans, donate cat or dog food to an animal shelter, or plant a tree in your backyard. Or start big: Get involved in a literacy program, start a food drive, or volunteer at an early childhood center. You might inspire others to follow your lead.

 **TODAY**

**I'll brainstorm ways I can make
a difference, then choose one to try.**

✪ JULY 13 ✪

"Family is just accident…. They don't mean
to get on your nerves. They don't even
mean to be your family, they just are."

Marsha Norman

Your parents nag you. Your siblings drive you crazy.
Your dad is always on your case; your mom wants to
run your life; your brother acts like he's king of the
world; your sister won't stay out of your room…. On
days when your family drives you crazy, consider what
life would be like without them. Who else would care
about your day? Give you a hug when you need it? Loan
you a sweatshirt or drive you to the mall? And love you
no matter what?

 **TODAY**

I'll cut my family some slack.

✪ JULY 14 ✪

"I think I should have no other mortal wants,
if I could always have plenty of music.
It seems to infuse strength into my limbs
and ideas into my brain. Life seems to go on
without effort, when I am filled with music."

George Eliot

Music is a source of expression, entertainment, and pleasure. Whether you listen to rock and roll, classical music, reggae, the blues, pop, gospel, jazz, or anything and everything, music can make you feel good all over. Make music part of your everyday life. You can sing, play an instrument, dance, write songs, or just listen. If you want to explore different types of music, find out if your local library lends CDs or tapes.

 **TODAY**

I'll play music.

"Dreams are renewable. No matter what
our age or condition, there are still
untapped possibilities within us
and new beauty waiting to be born."

Dale E. Turner

When you were younger, you might have dreamed of being a doctor, a pro basketball player, a teacher, a dancer, or any number of things. You might have dreamed about exploring the ocean floor or walking on the moon, discovering the cure for a terrible disease or writing a great book. What happened to that dream? Did it die a natural death because your goals and interests changed, or was it shoved aside because you decided it wasn't realistic? Or did someone else label your dream foolish, not good enough, or too good for you?

 **TODAY**

I'll renew a dream that matters to me.

✦ JULY 16 ✦

"It takes as much courage
to have tried and failed as it does
to have tried and succeeded."

Anne Morrow Lindbergh

Justine fastened the strap of her riding helmet and took a deep breath before climbing on her horse, Rascal. It was her first horse show, and she had to demonstrate trotting, cantering, and jumping. Rascal obeyed her commands until they reached the first jump—where he stopped short. Justine nudged his sides with her heels, shouted at him, and begged him to please just *move*. He didn't budge. Knowing she'd lost her chance for a ribbon, Justine was crushed. Afterward, her father reminded her that it took guts to try riding lessons, to participate in her first show—and to choose a horse with a name like Rascal. She knew he was right.

 **TODAY**

I'll recognize my courage.

"The pleasantest things in the world
are pleasant thoughts, and the great art of life
is to have as many of them as possible."

Montaigne

Why fill your head with gloom and doom? If your thoughts are dark and negative, it's hard to see the good things in your life—people who care about you, opportunities for learning and fun, a future as bright as you want it to be. Just for today, try banishing all sad, self-defeating thoughts from your mind. See how you feel at the end of the day. You might write about this experience in your journal—and pledge to do it again tomorrow.

 **TODAY**

I'll think pleasant thoughts.

"We will never have true civilization
until we have learned to recognize
the rights of others."

Will Rogers

When you're in a hurry or you have to wait, it's easy to forget you're part of the human race. You may be tempted to cut in line or cut someone off. You might lose your patience or lose your cool. You might give someone a hard time (or the finger). Slow down. Be patient. Take time to respect the rights of others.

 **TODAY**

I'll be patient with other people.

"I love to explore and taste and imagine."

Oliver Sacks

Summer is more than halfway over. Have you taken time to explore, taste, and imagine? Today might be a great day to stroll through a public garden, go to the zoo, or check out part of the library you don't usually visit (biographies? poetry? art history? architecture?). Or try out a new recipe or a new restaurant. Or grab a blanket, head for the park, find a quiet spot, and just daydream. Let your imagination wander wherever it wants to go.

TODAY

I'll explore.

"Family jokes, though rightly cursed
by strangers, are the bond that keeps
most families alive."

Stella Benson

Jokes, stories, tall tales, and legends—every family
has them. You might share yours over the dinner table,
during holidays, or at family reunions. Everyone has
a favorite or two, and what makes them special is
that they belong to your family and no one else. You
might even keep a Family Lore notebook. Whenever
something funny or memorable happens, jot it down.
Then, every so often, read parts aloud to your family.
People will love hearing them, no matter how often
they've heard them before.

TODAY

**I'll start collecting
family jokes and stories.**

"I like Bruce Lee, but I have my own style."

Jackie Chan

If you're a martial arts fan, you've probably seen a Jackie Chan movie. Today Jackie is a huge star, but he faced a challenge early in his career: He had to follow in the footsteps of the legendary Bruce Lee. When he tried, his films flopped. So he started to do things differently. "I looked at Bruce Lee movies," he said. "When he kicks high, I kick low." He also added touches of comedy. It's hard to follow in someone else's footsteps—those of an older sibling, last year's pitcher, the person who edited the yearbook before you. You have to find your own style.

TODAY

I'll do things my way.

⭐ JULY 22 ⭐

"Dare to be naive."

Buckminster Fuller

"You're *sooooo* naive." An insult…or a compliment? Buckminster Fuller was one of the 20th century's greatest and most original thinkers. He brought a childlike curiosity to all kinds of problems—how to shelter and feed people, how to combat industrial pollution, what to do about steadily decreasing world resources—and developed more than 2,000 patents along the way. You might have seen pictures of his famous Geodesic Dome in Montreal.

 **TODAY**

I'll be as curious as a child.

"It is the greatest shot of adrenaline
to be doing what you've wanted
to do so badly. You almost feel like
you could fly without the plane."

Charles Lindbergh

Accomplishing something that's important to you can feel like soaring among the clouds or walking on air. It's an adrenaline rush…a natural high. What would you like to achieve? Write a goal on a piece of paper, 3" x 5" card, or sticky note, then put it where you'll see it every day—as a reminder and a source of inspiration.

TODAY

I'll put a goal on paper.

✪ JULY 24 ✪

"If one is a greyhound,
why try to look like a Pekinese?"

Dame Edith Sitwell

Jordan wishes he looked like his best friend, Nick. Katie envies her friend Renee's curly hair. Renee longs to be taller and more muscular, like Katie. And Nick thinks he's not good-looking enough to ask Katie out on a date. It seems that nobody's happy with how they look. Are you? Why or why not?

 **TODAY**

I'll make a list of my best features.

"Another turning point, a fork stuck in
the road. Time takes you by the wrist,
directs you where to go."

Green Day

With so many choices before you, and so many deci-sions ahead of you, it's hard to feel secure. It might help to know that everyone else feels the same way at times, even adults. Living is a constant process of deciding what to do and where to go. And each choice you make helps you grow—and grow wiser. Have faith that your choices will lead you down the right path.

 **TODAY**

**I'll remember that insecurity
is part of life. And I'll trust myself
to make good decisions.**

"We expect more of ourselves
than we have any right to."

Oliver Wendell Holmes Jr.

Do you expect yourself to do everything right, never make a mistake, and please everyone on every try? It's time to crawl out of the "perfectionism pit" and see the light. Everyone makes errors, does a poor job once in a while, or fails completely. We all have flaws and things to learn. Let life be your teacher.

 **TODAY**

I won't expect myself to be perfect.

"The place to improve the world is first in one's own heart and head and hands."

Robert M. Pirsig

Marci is worried about the environment…but she doesn't conserve energy at home. Sean says he isn't a racist…but he laughs at the racist jokes his friends tell. Peter hates all the shootings in his city…but he spends his free time playing violent video games. Many people say one thing and do another—because it's easier, more comfortable, or they're going along with the crowd. If they really want to make the world a better place, maybe they need to start with themselves.

TODAY

I'll match my actions to my beliefs.

"Approach each new problem not with
a view of finding what you hope
will be there, but to get the truth."

Bernard M. Baruch

You see a problem one way; the other person sees it differently. You want to solve it your way; she (or he) has other ideas. Try this three-step problem-solving process:

1. *Recognize* the problem. Take turns expressing your feelings about it. Agree not to label or judge each other's feelings.
2. *Realize* you're part of the problem. Take responsibility for what you did or said. Agree that you want to solve the problem.
3. *Harmonize.* Work together to find a solution. Brainstorm possibilities without judging; be open to new ideas. Agree on a solution and act on it.

 **TODAY**

**I'll use this process
to solve a problem.**

☀ JULY 29 ☀

"Nobody sees a flower, really—it is so small—
we haven't time, and to see takes time,
like to have a friend takes time."

Georgia O'Keeffe

It takes a creative mind to make the connection between seeing a flower and having a friend. But what artist Georgia O'Keeffe said makes sense, if you stop to think about it. It takes time to notice the world around us—especially the things we usually take for granted. It takes time to have a friend—time spent together, having fun, talking, listening, and noticing when someone is happy or sad, stressed out or preoccupied. Is there someone in your life who deserves more of your time?

 **TODAY**

I'll make time for a friend.

"Those who are free of resentful thoughts
surely find peace."

The Buddha

Carla's parents divorced when she was twelve, and her
father moved out of the house. Carla was confused and
angry, and she blamed her parents for her misery. She
harbored her resentment, holding it close and allowing
it to grow stronger each day. She didn't realize that tending to her anger took all her time and energy, leaving
little room for other feelings—such as happiness,
excitement, love, enthusiasm, gratitude, or joy.

 **TODAY**

I'll let go of an old resentment.

✸ JULY 31 ✸

"Don't let other people tell you who you are."
Diane Sawyer

You are your own person. You are one-of-a-kind. There's no one else exactly like you (even if you're a twin). You have the power—and the right—to decide who you are, where you're going, and what you want your life to be. It's up to you.

 **TODAY**

I'll celebrate myself.

☼ AUGUST 1 ☼

"Don't let the fear of the time it will take
to accomplish something stand in the way
of your doing it. The time will pass anyway;
we might just as well put that passing time
to the best possible use."

Earl Nightingale

A woman once wrote to an advice columnist: "I'm thinking about going back to college and getting my degree. But it will take four years, and I'll be forty when I graduate!" The columnist replied: "How old will you be in four years if you don't graduate?" Time passes even when you're standing still. If there's something you really want to do—learn to play the trumpet, write a novel, restore an old car—don't worry how long it will take. The sooner you start, the sooner you'll reach your goal.

 **TODAY**

I'll start something I want to do.

"Friendship with oneself is all-important,
because without it one cannot
be friends with anyone else."

Eleanor Roosevelt

When you care about yourself, it's easier to care about
others. You feel better, stronger, and more positive, and
you're more willing to invite people to share your life.
Mark Twain put it this way: "The worst loneliness is not
to be comfortable with yourself." How can you be your
own best friend?

 **TODAY**

**I'll identify one way I can be
a better friend—to myself and others.**

☼ AUGUST 3 ☼

"Surround yourself with optimistic people."
Zig Ziglar

Divide a sheet of paper into two vertical columns. At the top of one column, write "Uppers." At the top of the other write "Downers." Now think of your friends—the people you hang out with. Who are the "uppers"—people who lift your spirits, encourage you, support you, and are generally positive and optimistic about life? And who are the "downers"—people who have something bad to say about everything (and everyone)? Write each person's name in the appropriate column. How do the two lists compare?

 **TODAY**

**I'll surround myself
with optimistic people.**

☼ AUGUST 4 ☼

"Eureka, I've found it!"

Archimedes

Doesn't it feel great to come up with a terrific idea? Or solve a problem? Or accomplish something? To keep those good feelings within reach, make a running list of your great ideas and achievements. If you want, call it your Eureka List. Store the list in your journal or backpack (or anywhere you like, so you can read it whenever you want and add to it anytime).

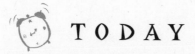 **TODAY**

I'll make a Eureka List.

☼ AUGUST 5 ☼

"A warm smile is the universal
language of kindness."

William Arthur Ward

Did you know it takes more muscles to frown than to smile? Smiling lifts your mood and brightens your outlook. And when you smile at people—friends and strangers alike—they can't help but feel good. Every year on the first Monday in August, National Smile week begins, and it lasts through the following Sunday. Practice your smile all this week—and for the rest of the year.

 **TODAY**

I'll smile.

"Some people think only intellect counts:
knowing how to solve problems, knowing
how to get by, knowing how to identify
an advantage and seize it. But the functions
of intellect are insufficient without courage,
love, friendship, compassion and empathy."

Dean Koontz

Courage, love, friendship, compassion, empathy: How
many of these qualities do you have? It's not enough
to be smart and successful. If you don't have courage,
you won't stick up for your beliefs; lacking love
and friendship, you'll be alone and lonely; without
compassion and empathy, any relationships you try to
form are doomed to fail. Take stock of yourself and your
character traits. Which ones do you need to work on
and strengthen? Who can help you?

 **TODAY**

**I'll be more loving...or I'll choose
another character trait to work on.**

☼ AUGUST 7 ☼

"Living is a form of not being sure,
not knowing what's next, or how."

Agnes B. de Mille

Which is why we must have faith in something. Some people have faith in God or another Higher Power; others trust themselves to find their own way. When you have faith, you feel more comfortable not knowing what comes next. As John Dewey once said, "To me, faith means not worrying."

 **TODAY**

I'll have faith.

"When we speak we echo many voices."

Mary Catherine Bateson

You may think that your thoughts, beliefs, and opinions are your own—that you formed them yourself without any help. But we're all influenced by people around us. If you've ever stuck up for yourself or defended a friend, spoken out about something important to you or taken a stand on an issue, where do you think that came from? Who in your life has helped you become a person of principles?

TODAY

**I'll make a list of the people
who have influenced me positively—
and choose one to thank.**

"The most important fact about
Spaceship Earth: an instruction book
didn't come with it."

Buckminster Fuller

Wouldn't it be easier if your life came with an instruction manual? Whenever you had questions, you could simply consult the instruction book and *voilà*, the answer would be right there in black and white— problem solved. You wouldn't have to cope with mistakes, failures, decisions, changes, doubts, and the unexpected. (On the other hand, there wouldn't be any surprises, either.)

 **TODAY**

I'll learn as I go.

✵ AUGUST 10 ✵

> "Whoever said anybody
> has a right to give up?"
>
> *Marian Wright Edelman*

As president and founder of the Children's Defense Fund, Marian Wright Edelman advocates for needy kids—poor and minority children, and those with disabilities—who can't vote, lobby, or speak for themselves. When Congress voted to cut $54 billion from welfare programs (including food stamp programs), it was a terrible blow. But Edelman refuses to give up. If you want to learn what the Children's Defense Fund is doing right now to help kids, check out the Web site: *www.childrensdefense.org*

TODAY

I won't give up on something that matters to me.

"What we need in the world is manners."

Eleanor Roosevelt

According to Alex J. Packer, author of *How Rude! The Teenagers' Guide to Good Manners, Proper Behavior, and Not Grossing People Out*, there are ten reasons why good manners are good for you. Here are the first five:

1. Good manners put people at ease.
2. Good manners impress people.
3. Good manners build self-esteem.
4. Good manners are attractive.
5. Good manners allow people to live and work together without unnecessary friction.

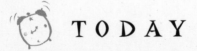 **TODAY**

I'll use good manners.

⚘ AUGUST 12 ⚘

"Good manners…are a priceless
insurance against failure and loneliness.
And anyone can have them."

Elsa Maxwell

Here are Alex J. Packer's next five reasons why good
manners are good for you:

6. Good manners can save your life. (How many
   kids and teens are shot because they
   "disrespected" someone with a gun?)
7. Good manners are rare. (Young people who
   have them sparkle like diamonds.)
8. Good manners make you feel good.
9. Good manners make others feel good.
10. Good manners don't cost anything.

 **TODAY**

**I'll keep using good manners.
(I might even make this a habit.)**

"When I feel low, I walk in the woods."

Sting

What do you do when you're unhappy, gloomy, or down? Do you have a special place you go, someone you like to talk to, or a journal that you write in? Any of these things can help make you feel better. When you're sad, do you cry? Or do you hold back your tears because you think crying is weird, babyish, stupid, or silly? Crying releases tension and pent-up emotions, and it can help you work through sadness, grief, or even anger. *Not* crying is like swallowing your pain and locking it inside you. Why not set it free?

 **TODAY**

I'll cheer myself up if I need it...
or cry if I want to.

"The best way to cheer yourself up is
to try to cheer somebody else up."

Mark Twain

On the way to visit their grandma in the hospital,
Michael sat in silence as his younger brother, Henry,
cried. They were both sad to learn about Grandma's
upcoming surgery. But when Henry was too upset to
enter the hospital room and kiss their grandma hello,
Michael knew he had to help. He marched in and
pretended he couldn't find Grandma anywhere, hoping
to make Henry smile. Grandma winked and played
along, calling out "Yoo hoo! Over here!" again and
again. Soon all three of them were laughing.

 **TODAY**

I'll spread good cheer.

☼ AUGUST 15 ☼

"One thing you can't recycle is wasted time."

Anonymous

Time's a-wasting, the clock is ticking, the hours are slipping away. Have you made time for something you really want to do? Don't put it off anymore. As Benjamin Franklin once said, "Lost time is never found again."

 **TODAY**

I'll make time for something special.

☼ AUGUST 16 ☼

"Being defeated is often a temporary condition.
Giving up is what makes it permanent."

Marilyn vos Savant

Madeleine L'Engle's book, *A Wrinkle in Time,* was
rejected by almost every major publisher before one
accepted it—after warning that the book probably
wouldn't sell. It won the Newbery Medal. Theodor
Geisel's first book, *And to Think That I Saw It on
Mulberry Street,* was rejected by 23 publishers. You
know Geisel by his pen name: Dr. Seuss. An editor once
told Louisa May Alcott that she would never write
anything people would buy; Alcott went on to write
Little Women. If you've enjoyed these authors' books,
aren't you glad they didn't give up?

 **TODAY**

**I won't let a past defeat
keep me from pursuing a goal.**

"Kids are the only future
the human race has."

William Saroyan

You're a citizen of your community, your nation, and the world. You have rights, a voice, and the power to make a difference. You're not too young to participate, to take action. What can you do to make the world a better place?

 **TODAY**

**I'll figure out one way
I can make a difference.**

"If you aim at nothing,
you'll meet it every time."

Anonymous

Some people find it difficult to set a goal. They're afraid to take a risk. Or they believe that if they don't aim for anything, they won't fail or be disappointed. In the words of Frederick Wilcox, "You can't steal second base and keep your foot on first."

 **TODAY**

I'll set a reachable goal for myself.

"Each problem that I solved
became a rule which served afterwards
to solve other problems."

René Descartes

Problem solving is a skill you learn, not an ability you're born with. Like any other skill, it takes practice. Sometimes you'll succeed, and sometimes you'll fail. If you want to learn from your successes (and your failures), you might want to keep a problem-solving notebook. Jot down the problems you're facing, how you plan to solve them, and whether or not your efforts worked. (See pages 210 and 278–279 for problem-solving strategies.) You'll have a history you can use to solve other problems.

 **TODAY**

I'll start a problem-solving notebook.

"I respect my body and make changes
in it to help me achieve my goals."

Rebecca Lobo

Quick Quiz: Exercise can:

(A) burn body fat

(B) improve your metabolism

(C) make you look better and healthier

(D) all of the above.

If you guessed D, you're right. Exercise does all that and more. When you work out regularly, you can also expect these kinds of rewards: stronger bones and joints, leaner muscles, and better self-esteem.

 **TODAY**

I'll work out.

"If you are bored, then it is
boring to be with you."

Sol Gordon

"If you are bored," professor and author Sol Gordon goes on to say, "don't announce it. It is especially unattractive to bemoan how you don't like yourself, or that you have 'nothing to do.' If you have nothing to do, don't do it in company." There's an alternative to being bored and boring: Be interested and interesting. Find *something* that sparks your curiosity, gets you excited, or makes you want to know more. Enthusiasm can erase boredom, plus it's a people magnet.

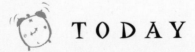 **TODAY**

I won't be boring.

"I don't think life should ever exceed your dreams, because then you stop dreaming."

Michelle Williams

Michelle Williams had her first big-screen acting role when she was a 14-year-old high school freshman, playing the part of April in the 1994 remake of *Lassie*. Since then, she has appeared in more movies (*A Thousand Acres, Halloween H2O*) and starred as Jen Lindley on *Dawson's Creek*. And she's still dreaming.

 **TODAY**

I'll dream big dreams.

"Worry never dried a tear,
worry never calmed a fear."

Anonymous

Are you a worrywart? Is your mind always full of what ifs? (*What if I'm not good enough? What if I can't do it? What if something goes wrong? What if someone criticizes me? What if I fail?*) Often the things we worry about never even happen. And when they do, they're not as bad as we feared they would be.

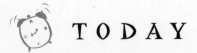 **TODAY**

I'll let go of a worry.

☼ AUGUST 24 ☼

"Without risks, there is
no chance for rewards."

Richard Bangs

To get where you want to go in life, you'll have to take risks. Not stupid, reckless, impetuous risks, but planned, thought-out, *reasonable* risks—ones where the chance of something good happening is greater than the chance of something bad happening. Risking and succeeding builds optimism and confidence. Risking and failing builds resilience; you learn to deal with frustration and failure. Either way, you win!

 **TODAY**

I'll plan to take a risk.

"Among my most prized possessions
are the words that I have never spoken."

Orson Rega Card

Thoughtless words, careless words, words said in anger
or to get back at someone—those are better left unspo-
ken. If you have a tendency to open mouth, insert foot,
today might be a good day to start doing something
about it. This isn't being dishonest; it's being tactful
and kind. Words can hurt as much as fists, and why
would you want to hurt another person? How does that
benefit you?

 **TODAY**

I'll think before I speak.

☼ AUGUST 26 ☼

"The voyage of discovery lies not in finding new landscapes, but in having new eyes."

Marcel Proust

Have you ever considered running away? Maybe you've actually done it once or twice. Many teens have family struggles or personal problems that seem overwhelming and impossible to handle—you're not alone. But running away creates its own set of problems, and they may be a lot more serious than the ones you're trying to escape. Before you start packing, talk with an adult you trust. If you don't have anyone to talk to, call a crisis hotline. The Girls and Boys Town National Hotline has highly trained, professional, sympathetic counselors available 24 hours a day, 7 days a week. Call 1-800-448-3000.

 **TODAY**

**I'll look at my problems
with fresh eyes. If I need help,
I'll find it.**

☼ AUGUST 27 ☼

"So hold on to the ones who really care.
In the end they'll be the only ones there."

Hanson

Who are the people in your life who care about you the most? Probably your parents, siblings, relatives, and friends. How can you show you care in return? If you're comfortable giving someone a hug and saying "I love you," do so. If that's not your thing, you could send a letter, card, or email to express your feelings. Perhaps you could do a special favor for someone you love—even anonymously, if you wish. Let people know how much they mean to you. It will make their day (and yours).

 **TODAY**

I'll show someone I care.

"You will never find time for anything.
You must make it."

Charles Buxton

As you start the school year, one of the best things you can do for yourself is to *get organized*. Buy a daily planner from an office supplies store, then learn how to use it. Some come with instructions; if yours doesn't, talk to an adult who uses a planner and get tips from him or her. Here are some things you'll want to write in your planner throughout the year:

- appointments (doctor, dentist, etc.)
- assignments (homework, long-term assignments—and steps)
- commitments (tutoring, volunteering, etc.)
- extracurricular activities
- Things to Do lists.

 **TODAY**

**I'll buy a daily planner
and learn how to use it.**

"Fall seven times, stand up eight."

Japanese proverb

If you've ever watched a boxing match, you've seen the opponents endure blow after blow but continue to stand and fight. Have you ever felt like you've been tossed into the ring and battered from all sides? There will be many tough times in your life; you may lose a loved one, get sick, or have to deal with family problems, a move, or other stressful events. You can't avoid difficulties, but you can meet them with courage and strength. Stand strong, and if you need help, reach out to someone you trust. You don't have to face the fight alone.

 **TODAY**

**I'll make a list of people
I can talk to during tough times.**

"At first people refuse to believe that a strange
new thing can be done, and then they begin
to hope it can be done, then they see it can
be done…then it is done and all the world
wonders why it was not done centuries ago."

Frances Hodgson Burnett

At one time, people didn't believe humans could fly—
until the Wright brothers proved them wrong. Imagine
the world without air travel or space exploration…or
cars, computers, antibiotics, telephones, and all the
other inventions that once were unfathomable. Where
would we be without visionaries—those who are able to
see far beyond what most other people see?

 **TODAY**

I'll keep my mind open to possibilities.

"Self-respect permeates
every aspect of your life."

Joe Clark

Self-respect means that you don't take foolish risks. You stick up for yourself and defend your values and beliefs. You take good care of your body and your health; you don't risk harming it with alcohol or other drugs. If you have self-respect, it really *does* permeate every aspect of your life; your goals, your decisions, the choices you make, the people you hang out with and the things you do. If you don't have self-respect, building it should be your #1 goal.

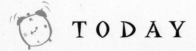 **TODAY**

I'll respect myself.

★ SEPTEMBER 1 ★

"Where there is life, there is hope.
Where there are hopes, there are dreams.
Where there are vivid dreams repeated,
they become goals."

Denis Waitley

When you dream about your future, perhaps you see yourself piloting jumbo jets around the world. You hear the sounds of the engines, see the control panels, imagine soaring over clouds and through skies of infinite blue.... Dream vividly, in as much detail as you can. When you want more details, seek them out. Read books about flying. Interview a pilot and write an article for your school newspaper. Request information from flight schools. Find out what it takes to become a pilot—and plan how you'll do it. Now you've got a goal.

 **TODAY**

I'll start turning a dream into a goal.

★ SEPTEMBER 2 ★

"Nothing should be prized more highly
than the value of each day."

Johann von Goethe

How will you prize the value of this day? What will you do to make it count? Maybe this is the day to start a big project, say hi to someone you'd like to know, strengthen a friendship, find a mentor, sign up for a class, take a positive risk, join a club, volunteer for a service project, tell your parents you love them, start a fitness program, break a bad habit, or...?

 **TODAY**

I'll make the most of the day.

★ SEPTEMBER 3 ★

> "The teenage years: who needs 'em? We're sitting around minding our own business and suddenly our bodies go berserk."
>
> *Kaz Cooke*

One day you're just a kid; the next your hormones are out of control, and all sorts of embarrassing things start to happen. You sweat more than ever. Hairs spring up everywhere. Certain body parts get bigger. Zits attack your face. Arrrgggh! Puberty is uncomfortable, but it's also perfectly normal. If you're having trouble coping, talk to a friend, an older sibling, a parent, or someone else you trust. (And if you're concerned that everyone but you is experiencing these changes, don't worry—your time will come.)

 **TODAY**

I'll remember that puberty happens to everyone.

★ SEPTEMBER 4 ★

"You may think that your talents or gifts are small, but you can work hard to nurture them. You will achieve success if you believe in yourself, strive for the best, and never give up."

Cassandra Walker

Some people are born with a talent they discover when they're very young. You may have heard of child prodigies who perform with orchestras, attend college, or patent inventions before they're in their teens. For most of us, our gifts aren't as obvious. If you haven't found your talents yet, don't despair. We all have *something* we're good at. Do you write great essays in English? Maybe you're destined to be an author. Do have a knack for oral reports? Maybe public speaking is in your future. Do you enjoy fixing things around the house? You could end up building homes someday.

 **TODAY**

I'll nurture my talents.

★ SEPTEMBER 5 ★

"If you judge people,
you have no time to love them."

Mother Teresa

Mother Teresa, a recipient of the Nobel Peace Prize, crossed all boundaries of race and religion to feed the hungry, aid the poor, and comfort those in need. She was a living symbol of kindness, devotion, and unconditional love. She once said "If I love until it hurts, then there is no hurt, but only more love." Mother Teresa died on this day in 1997 and was mourned around the world.

 **TODAY**

I'll love unconditionally.

★ SEPTEMBER 6 ★

"If you don't ask, you don't get."

Mohandas Gandhi

You can wish that your teacher would take time to explain assignments more clearly. You can hope that your parents will give you more freedom. You can want your friends to listen when you need to talk. And you can wait…and wait…and wait for everyone you know to become a mind reader. Asking is faster!

 TODAY

I'll ask for what I need.

★ SEPTEMBER 7 ★

"Comparison is a death knell
to sibling harmony."

Elisabeth Fishel

Nobody likes being compared to somebody else—especially when the comparison isn't favorable. (*Examples:* "Why can't you be more responsible, like your sister?" Or "Your brother got A's all the way through high school. Why can't you?") Comparing siblings is a surefire way to create family disharmony. If your parents are comparers, this might be a good topic for a family meeting. You and your siblings could tell your parents how you feel about being compared, and everyone could brainstorm ways to encourage each other without comparing. (For family meeting tips, see page 58.)

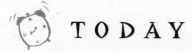 **TODAY**

**I won't compare myself
to my sibling(s).**

★ SEPTEMBER 8 ★

"The number one indicator of success
for a child is a good relationship
with a caring adult."

Fortune magazine

A 1995 study for Big Brothers Big Sisters of America found that young people with mentors are 46 percent less likely to use illegal drugs, 27 percent less likely to start using alcohol, 53 percent less likely to skip school, and more confident of their school performance. Plus they get along better with their families. According to a 1989 Louis Harris Poll, 59 percent of mentored teens get better grades and 73 percent raise their goals. If you don't have a mentor, maybe it's time to find one.

 **TODAY**

**I'll think seriously
about finding a mentor.**

★ SEPTEMBER 9 ★

"A mentor is any caring adult who makes
an active, positive contribution to the life
of a child who is not his or her own."

The Points of Light Foundation

Where can you find a mentor? In your neighborhood, at school, in the workplace, in your congregation, at a recreation center or community center, where your parents work, at a youth service organization (*examples:* Big Brothers Big Sisters, the YMCA/YWCA, Boy Scouts, Girl Scouts, Boys Clubs, Girls, Inc.), and almost anywhere else caring adults are likely to be. Learn more (*much* more) about finding a mentor by contacting: MENTOR/The National Mentoring Partnership, 1600 Duke Street, Suite 300, Alexandria, VA 22314; (703) 224-2200. On the Web, go to: *www.mentoring.org*

 **TODAY**

**I'll take the first step(s)
toward finding a mentor.**

★ SEPTEMBER 10 ★

"There are three kinds of people:
those who watch what happens,
those who wonder what happened,
and those who make things happen.
Which are you?"

Charles A. Mann

Do you want to make things happen? Then be active and get involved. Join a club, volunteer, contribute to a worthy cause, write a letter to your congressperson, try out for a sport or the school play, start a business, or run for a class office. Don't just be a watcher or a wonderer.

 TODAY

I'll make something happen.

★ SEPTEMBER 11 ★

> "Research is what I'm doing
> when I don't know what I'm doing."
>
> *Werner von Braun*

Are you a good researcher? If you need the answer to a question, can you find it? Ask a librarian to show you around the library's resources. (This will take a while, so call ahead and make an appointment.) Ask someone who's Internet savvy to take you on a tour of cyberspace. Learn about organizations, agencies, and sources you can contact. Knowing how to research is important to your school success—but it's more than that. You'll use these skills for a lifetime.

 **TODAY**

I'll become a better researcher.

★ SEPTEMBER 12 ★

"I only remember one B in my life. The rest were a few C's, mostly D's, and lots and lots and lots of F's. But I always believed in myself. This came from knowing that there were other things that I could do better than anyone else."

Dr. John (Jack) Horner

All through his school years, Jack Horner got terrible grades, and he even flunked out of college. Today he's a brilliant paleontologist at the top of his field. He was the real-life model for the paleontologist in the movie *Jurassic Park,* and he has received a MacArthur Foundation Award (also known as a Genius Award). If your grades aren't the greatest, talk to your parents and teachers. Do you need a tutor? Can you join a study group? What other options do you have?

 **TODAY**

I'll plan ways to be more successful in school.

> "The future belongs to those who
> believe in the beauty of their dreams."

Eleanor Roosevelt

Do you believe dreams come true? Merrick Johnston does. At age 12, she became the youngest person to climb to the summit of Alaska's Mt. McKinley, the tallest mountain in North America. To accomplish this feat, she battled nerves, cold, and exhaustion, telling herself again and again *"I can do it."* What heights do you dream of climbing?

 **TODAY**

I'll believe in my dreams.

★ SEPTEMBER 14 ★

"Violence is, essentially, a confession
of ultimate inarticulateness."

Time magazine

In a series of incidents in 1997 and 1998, children armed with guns shot and killed other children—and teachers—at schools across the country. A stunned nation asked "Why?" but there are no easy answers. Even though school violence is on the rise, you don't have to feel like a victim (or potential victim). Do your part to open the lines of communication at your school. Talk about violence—how it relates to your school and what everyone can do to prevent it. Does your school have a no-tolerance policy about violence and weapons? Do students and teachers feel safe?

 TODAY

**I'll work to make my school
safer for everyone.**

"Opportunity may knock only once,
but temptation leans on the doorbell."

Anonymous

Sex, alcohol and other drugs, smoking, hanging out with the wrong crowd...the teen years are full of temptations. What will you do? That depends on factors including:

- how you were raised
- your moral, ethical, and/or religious values
- your self-esteem (do you respect yourself enough to say no to temptation and peer pressure?)
- your long-term vs. short-term concerns (are you living only in the present, or planning for your future?)
- your common sense.

Are you ready to make decisions that will help you instead of hurting you?

 **TODAY**

**I'll think through what
I'll do when I'm tempted.**

★ SEPTEMBER 16 ★

"When you're going through hell,
don't stop!"

Trevor Romain

Sometimes you might feel like the sky is falling—like your world is crashing down around you. Instead of getting buried beneath the rubble, pick yourself up, dust yourself off, and keep going. If you feel like you've reached the limits of what you can handle, talk to an adult you trust. Allow a parent, teacher, counselor, or clergy member to give you a helping hand.

 **TODAY**

**If I'm struggling,
I'll find the help I need.**

"How very little can be done
under the spirit of fear."

Florence Nightingale

Fear can feel like a wild animal breathing down your neck. When you're scared, your heart and thoughts race, your palms sweat, you breathe rapidly, and you may get butterflies in your stomach. All of these physical and mental reactions, though normal, can make it hard to cope. If you're scared about something, take several long, slow, deep breaths. Once you feel calmer (and you will), you'll be in a better position to handle your fear.

TODAY

I'll breathe slowly and deeply.

"I generally think people are special....
I need to give them the courtesy
of being decent."

David Robinson

David Robinson, the All-Star center for the San Antonio Spurs, is a Naval Academy graduate, born-again Christian, and two-time Olympic gold medalist who doesn't do drugs, talk trash, or get rude when fans ask for his autograph. "The Admiral" could be a jerk (he wouldn't be the first sports star to go that route), but instead he's a role model and a philanthropist, giving generously to help schools, children's charities, and the homeless. Despite his stardom, fame, and reputation, he insists that he's "just a normal person."

 **TODAY**

**I'll treat people with
courtesy and respect.**

★ SEPTEMBER 19 ★

"No matter how good you are,
you have to work hard, or you'll
only be as funny as the next guy."

Chris Rock

You won the election. You got the part. You aced the test. You scored the winning point. Now what? Savor your success for a while...then get back to work! No matter how good you are, there's probably room for improvement. And the only way to keep your skills sharp is to use them. (P.S. Comedian and actor Chris Rock dropped out of high school—but later earned his G.E.D.)

 **TODAY**

I'll keep working.

"Fight fire with fire,
and all you'll end up with is ashes."

Abigail Van Buren ("Dear Abby")

Someone punched you, so you punched back—and now you're in trouble at school. Your parents yelled at you, so you yelled back—and now you're in trouble at home. A friend insulted you, so you said something even worse to her—and now you wonder if your friendship has been damaged beyond repair. Losing your temper, blowing your stack, getting back at someone who hurt you…it may feel right at the time, but it almost always makes things worse.

 **TODAY**

I'll keep my temper under control.

"Often the best way to win is
to forget to keep score."

Marianne Espinosa Murphy

You paid for dinner the last time you and a friend went out, so next time it's her turn, right? Or you did the dishes for your brother yesterday, so today he should take out the trash for you. Give-and-take is an important part of any relationship, but you can't always count on an equal exchange. And if you expect something back for every favor you do, you're going to be resentful when that doesn't happen. Sometimes it's best not to keep score.

 **TODAY**

**I'll do a favor without
expecting anything in return.**

"It's one thing to say, 'I know I'm attractive.
I know I'm this or that.' It's another thing
to love the way you feel inside and the way
the world looks at you, no matter
what your flaws are."

Forest Whitaker

The appearance of self-confidence can hide a pile of anxieties. The most popular and successful person you know might be struggling with doubts and serious problems. You've probably seen or read news reports about teens who seemed to have everything—intelligence, accomplishments, looks, loving families, close friends, bright futures—yet they killed themselves. They didn't love themselves enough to want to live.

 **TODAY**

I'll love myself in spite of my flaws.

★ SEPTEMBER 23 ★

"Winning isn't everything. Wanting to win is."

Catfish Hunter

To succeed in school (and in life), you need to be motivated from the *inside,* not the outside. Rewards (parents who pay you for A's, teachers who give special privileges) and punishments (parents who ground you for D's, teachers who withhold privileges) are external motivations. If you're motivated from the outside, you're likely to choose the fastest, easiest ways to learn…and you won't learn much.

 **TODAY**

I'll be motivated from the inside.

★ SEPTEMBER 24 ★

"Guard well your spare moments.
They are like uncut diamonds. Discard
them and their value will never be known.
Improve them and they will become
the brightest gems in a useful life."

Ralph Waldo Emerson

You have a little time before dinner, so you decide to watch TV. There's nothing good on, but you aimlessly flip from channel to channel anyway. Before long, you feel like a total couch potato and you're annoyed at yourself, the TV, and everything else. Your spare moments can add up to time well spent, but only if you make the most of them. You might use your free time to email your grandpa, catch up on your homework, read, walk the dog, or pitch in with dinner. See how much you can accomplish when you use those moments wisely.

 **TODAY**

I'll make the most of my free time.

"It gets dark sometimes, but morning comes.... Keep hope alive."

Jesse Jackson

Daylight fades; night falls. Then it's morning, and the sun rises once again, bringing warmth and light. You know this will happen, just as you know the ocean tides will ebb and flow. It's all part of the rhythm of life. When you're sad, or when your days are dark, remember that morning will come. Darkness doesn't last forever.

 **TODAY**

I'll remember that sadness passes.

★ SEPTEMBER 26 ★

"In preparing for battle I have
always found that plans are useless,
but planning is indispensable."

Dwight D. Eisenhower

Are you a good planner? Take this quiz and find out.
Answer each question yes, no, or sometimes.

1. Do you make daily plans?
2. Do you write your plans down?
3. Are your plans flexible?
4. Do you review your plans at the end of the day?

SCORING: The more yes answers, the better. If most
of your answers were sometimes or no, how can you
plan to change that? P.S. Even if your plans don't turn
out the way you want, you'll still benefit from the
process of planning. You'll be more prepared for whatever happens.

 **TODAY**

I'll be a better planner.

"The secret to succeeding is inner strength."

Shaquille O'Neal

During a storm, trees are lashed by wind and driving rain. Watch what happens. The trees will bend and sway, but once the storm is over, they'll stand tall again. Trees have deep roots that hold fast to the earth. You can't see the roots, but they're there beneath the surface, supporting the tree and growing stronger as time passes. Like a tree, you have a support system—your inner strength. It can help you weather storms.

 **TODAY**

I'll rely on my inner strength.

"I slept and dreamt that life was pleasure,
I woke and saw that life was service,
I served and discovered that service
was pleasure."

Rabindranath Tagore

When Independent Sector (a national organization) surveyed teenagers who volunteer to help others, they learned something interesting: The teens reported gaining specific *benefits* from giving service. Here are the Top 5:

1. They learned to respect others.
2. They learned to be helpful and kind.
3. They learned how to get along with and relate to others.
4. They gained satisfaction from helping others.
5. They learned to understand people who are different from them.

 **TODAY**

I'll start looking for ways to serve.

★ SEPTEMBER 29 ★

"I don't know what your destiny will be,
but one thing I do know: the only ones
among you who will be really happy are those
who have sought and found how to serve."

Albert Schweitzer

Teens surveyed by Independent Sector reported five more benefits of serving others:

6. They learned how to relate to younger children.
7. They became better people.
8. They learned new skills.
9. They developed leadership skills.
10. They became more patient with others.

You can get involved with a local or national service organization. Ask a youth leader, teacher, community leader, or religious leader for suggestions. Or maybe your school offers service learning opportunities. What would you like to do?

 TODAY

**I'll gather information
about service organizations.**

"Service is the rent that you pay
for room on this earth."

Shirley Chisholm

The first black woman elected to the U.S. House of Representatives, Shirley Chisholm served the people for seven terms, often speaking up for the urban poor. She's not the only wise person who has insisted that service is a duty, not a choice. Marian Wright Edelman once said: "Service is the rent we pay for living." And Eleanor Roosevelt put it this way: "Usefulness, whatever form it may take, is the price we should pay for the air we breathe and the food we eat and the privilege of being alive."

 **TODAY**

**I'll make a real commitment
to serve others—either through
an organization or on my own.**

"If someone had told me I would be Pope
one day, I would have studied harder."

Pope John Paul I

Why study literature? Who needs math? Why should you care about history, biology, Spanish, or grammar? It's tempting to slack off in classes that seem irrelevant. In a recent Public Agenda survey of more than 1,300 high school students, 65 percent admitted they could do much better in school if they tried. Any knowledge—all knowledge—is potentially valuable to you, even if it doesn't make sense right now. You won't be in school forever. Why not learn as much as you can while you're there?

 **TODAY**

I'll study harder.

"Just as the hand, held before the eye,
can hide the tallest mountain, so the routine
of everyday life can keep us from seeing
the vast radiance of and the secret
wonders that fill the world."

Hassidic saying

You shower, dress, eat, run out the door, attend class, and go to sports or lessons. Followed by chores, dinner, homework, and on and on and on. Each day, you probably follow a familiar routine that keeps you busy and fills up most of your time. But do you ever take a moment to enjoy the beauty that surrounds you? Watch a bird soaring in the sky or building its nest, lie back and gaze at the clouds, observe the sun rising or setting, or look for the constellations at night.

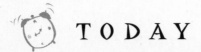 **TODAY**

I'll enjoy nature's beauty.

☾ OCTOBER 3 ☾

"We have as much time as we need."

Melody Beattie

If you don't have time for things that are important to you, it's time to take a look at your schedule. Make a list of your commitments—including chores, activities, lessons, and any clubs, teams, and organizations you belong to. Add to that list anything you really *want* to do but haven't been able to fit in. (Don't forget "have fun.") Circle the commitments you'd like to let go—and be ruthless. Talk with your parents; their ideas about what you should do might differ from yours, and it's worth hearing their side.

 **TODAY**

I'll review my schedule
and make any needed changes.

"If the only tool you have is a hammer,
you tend to see every problem as a nail."

Abraham Maslow

To solve problems effectively, you need a variety of tools in your problem-solving toolbox. Try a technique called Creative Problem Solving (CPS for short). Developed by Dr. Alex Osborn and Dr. Sidney Parnes, this famous five-step process has helped all kinds of people solve all kinds of problems. Here are the steps:

1. Determine the facts. (Be specific.)
2. Analyze the problem. (Ask questions. Gather information. Review what you learn.)
3. Brainstorm potential solutions. (Be creative.)
4. Evaluate potential solutions. (What might happen if…?)
5. Select and carry out a solution.

 **TODAY**

I'll use CPS to solve a problem.

☾ OCTOBER 5 ☾

"Creativity can solve almost any problem.
The creative act, the defeat of habit
by originality, overcomes everything."

George Lois

Try these tips to improve your CPS (Creative Problem
Solving) skills:

1. If you think of a great solution before finishing
   all five steps in the CPS process, stop and try it.
2. If you get stuck or run into new problems, start
   over with step 1 to gain a fresh perspective.
3. Brainstorming is most effective when you do it
   in a group. Ask your family or friends to join you.
4. Don't get frustrated if CPS doesn't work for you
   right away. Like anything else worth doing well,
   CPS takes practice.
5. Have fun! Remember that CPS is *creative*
   problem solving.

 **TODAY**

I'll practice my CPS skills.

"One of the messages that I have for people
who are sick or going through tough times
in other areas of their lives is, do not give up."

Michelle Akers

Michelle Akers, a world champion soccer player
and Olympic gold medalist, relies on her strength,
determination, and endurance to score goals and be a
winner. These qualities are regularly put to the test both
on and off the field because Michelle has chronic
fatigue syndrome, an illness that leaves her exhausted
and extremely weak. If you're ill, coping with grief, or
handling a problem, believe that you can face it with
courage and determination. Don't give up.

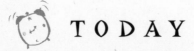 **TODAY**

I won't give up.

☾ OCTOBER 7 ☾

"The trouble with not having a goal is
that you can spend your life running up
and down the field and never scoring."

Bill Copeland

Do you sometimes feel that your life has no purpose or
meaning? That you're not accomplishing much, even
though you're always busy? As if you're running and
running but never quite getting anywhere? Goals make
it possible for you to get somewhere. If you want more
control over your life, start by setting at least one *long-
range goal*—something important and meaningful
you'd like to accomplish within the next three to six
months. Next, come up with three *short-range goals* that
will help you reach your long-range goal. Break your
short-range goals into steps…and get started.

 TODAY

**I'll set one long-range goal
and three short-range goals
that will help me reach it.**

*"Don't sweat the small stuff…
and it's all small stuff."*

Richard Carlson

You miss the bus, say something stupid in French class, and stub your toe at soccer practice. Then, on the way home, you realize you've forgotten the book you need for your English assignment. How do you react? You can get upset and blow up, or you can laugh it off and say "No big deal. I'll get through this." You can go home, slam the door to your bedroom, and tell your family that you hate your life—or you can go home, tell your family all the silly things that happened, and let them laugh along with you. Which do you think feels better?

 **TODAY**

I won't blow things out of proportion.

☾ OCTOBER 9 ☾

"I am never afraid of what I know."

Anna Sewell

You thought he was your friend—then you learned he was talking behind your back. You thought she would keep your secret—then you found out she was spreading it all over school. Knowledge can be painful; it hurts to discover you were wrong about someone you believed in (or something you believed). When you have the facts, you can make informed decisions and better choices. Don't close your ears or your mind to the truth, even when you wish things were different.

 **TODAY**

I won't fear the truth.

⸨ OCTOBER 10 ⸩

"Learning…should be a joy
and full of excitement."

Taylor Caldwell

Are you having a problem with a class or an assignment? Do you sometimes feel that school is a waste
of your time? Do you have ideas for making school
better? Don't just tell your friends. Talk to the teacher.
Here's how:

1. Make an appointment to meet and talk. This
   shows the teacher you're serious.
2. Think through what you want to say ahead
   of time. Make a list of the things you want to
   cover and bring it to the meeting.
3. Choose your words carefully. Don't blame,
   complain, or accuse. Ask questions, make
   suggestions, and offer solutions.

 **TODAY**

I'll decide if I should talk to a teacher.

"I have learned a great deal from listening
carefully. Most people never listen."

Ernest Hemingway

Here are three more tips for talking to teachers:

4. Be respectful. Teachers have feelings, too.
5. Bring your sense of humor. Be willing to laugh
    at your own misunderstandings and mistakes.
6. Don't forget to listen. The purpose of your
    meeting isn't to hear yourself talk. You can do
    that on your own time.

What if your meeting isn't successful? Ask another adult
for help. "Successful" doesn't necessarily mean getting
everything you want. You might have to compromise.

 **TODAY**

**If I need to talk to a teacher,
I'll make an appointment.**

"You can't have a better tomorrow if you are thinking about yesterday all the time."

Charles F. Kettering

Some people look back at the past and see only the things they should have done (or wish they hadn't done). Others long for the way things used to be. Either way, they're stuck—in regret or nostalgia. It's good to learn from the past, but don't get trapped there. Should haves, could haves, and would haves can tie you down. If there's something you *can* change, go ahead and change it. If there's something you *can't* change, admit it and move on with your life.

 **TODAY**

I'll get over it.

☾ OCTOBER 13 ☾

"The truly educated never graduate."

Bumper sticker

Janice is learning to speak Spanish. Raoul is taking a painting class. Tom and Bev just signed up for an accounting course. Would it surprise you to learn that all four of these people are adults? If you love learning, it doesn't stop when you graduate from high school or college. If you don't love learning, you have a problem. Lifelong learning keeps your brain in shape. It makes you more attractive to employers. It makes you more interested in life—and more interesting to be around.

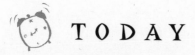 **TODAY**

I'll love learning.

❰ OCTOBER 14 ❰

"I've always believed that you can funnel good things toward yourself by positive thinking."

Jim Carrey

Optimists are positive thinkers. They look on the sunny side of life, they're cheerful and enthusiastic, and they believe in the power of laughter. Are you familiar with the Optimist Clubs? Since the early 1900s, these clubs have worked on behalf of youth, promoting leadership, volunteerism, and service (you can learn more online at *www.optimist.org*). Part of the Optimist Creed is to "think only of the best, to work only for the best, and to expect only the best." Can you make this promise to yourself?

TODAY

I'll do my best to expect the best.

⊂ OCTOBER 15 ⊂

"Know the true value of time; snatch, seize,
and enjoy every moment of it. No idleness;
no laziness; no procrastination; never put off
till tomorrow what you can do today."

Lord Chesterfield

There's something you're supposed to do, but you just can't make yourself do it. It's too big, too overwhelming, too whatever. Stop torturing yourself and just do it! Break it down into steps. Then choose a *specific* date and time when you'll work on the first step. If you use a daily planner, write it there. You've just made an appointment with yourself. Plan to spend at least 15 minutes a day working through the steps until you're done.

TODAY

I'll tackle a task I've been avoiding.

☾ OCTOBER 16 ☾

> "To make a difference is not
> a matter of accident, a matter of
> casual occurrence of the tides.
> People choose to make a difference."
>
> *Maya Angelou*

There are so many ways to make a difference in other people's lives. If you want, you can start small. Try smiling at someone in school—someone you don't usually notice, maybe someone who isn't especially popular. Or start bigger. Call your local Red Cross or Habitat for Humanity chapter—or any other organization you're interested in—and offer to volunteer. Join a service club at school, in your community, or in your congregation. Make the choice to make a difference.

 **TODAY**

**I'll make a difference in
at least one person's life.**

> "Don't get your knickers in a knot.
> Nothing is solved and it
> just makes you walk funny."
>
> *Kathryn Carpenter*

Laura was sitting at the table eating breakfast when her little sister, Stacy, walked in wearing Laura's favorite shirt. Furious, Laura screamed "Take it off!" When Stacy refused, Laura reached out to grab her and accidently knocked her bowlful of cereal across the table. Both Laura and Stacy ended up covered in milk and had to change their clothes; by the time the bus arrived, the sisters weren't on speaking terms. As they rode to school, they happened to look at each other at the same moment—and burst out laughing.

 **TODAY**

I'll lighten up.

❝ OCTOBER 18 ❝

> "My errors were more fertile
> than I ever imagined."
>
> *Jan Tschichold*

Cheese. Chocolate chip cookies. Coca-Cola. Penicillin. Post-it Notes. Silly Putty. The yo-yo. Dynamite. What do they have in common? All were discovered or invented by mistake. According to authors Judy Galbraith and Jim Delisle, there are at least five reasons why misteaks are grate. Here are the first three:

1. Mistakes are universal. Everybody makes them.
2. Mistakes show that you're learning. They inspire you to do better next time.
3. Mistakes show that you're trying something new or different.

 **TODAY**

I won't be afraid to make a mistake.

"People fail forward to success."

Mary Kay Ash

Here are a couple more reasons why mistayks are bennifishul:

4. Mistakes allow you to see your own improvements. Are you a better bike rider, basketball player, singer, painter, trumpet player, speller, scientist, or whatever than you were last year? You can't get better if you're afraid to goof up.

5. Mistakes allow you to learn from others. If you have a problem you're trying to solve, you don't have to go it alone. You can ask for help. And if you think that no one will help you, you're probably...mistaken.

 **TODAY**

**I'll remember a time when
I learned from a mistake.**

"Without ambition one starts nothing.
Without work one finishes nothing."

Ralph Waldo Emerson

Do you begin new activities with a burst of enthusiasm, then get bored and say "Forget it"? Is your room full of half-finished books, photos you're "getting around to" putting in your album, a not-quite-done science project, a musical instrument you no longer play, unused exercise equipment, empty journals you've been meaning to fill? Some people are good starters but not necessarily good finishers (and some people have a hard time starting at all). It may be hard work to see a project to completion, but it's worth the effort.

 **TODAY**

I'll finish something.

> "Every family is a 'normal' family....
> Wherever there is lasting love,
> there is a family."
>
> *Shere Hite*

Families today come in all shapes and sizes. Two parents, one parent, divorced parents, stepparents, foster parents, grandparents, kids, adopted kids, foster kids...even among your friends, you're likely to find a wide variety. In most cases, it's no longer shameful or embarrassing to have a family that doesn't fit the so-called "ideal" (dad + mom + 2.5 kids). What matters most is whether you love each other.

 **TODAY**

I'll appreciate my family.

"What happens to you when you get hooked on drugs or drink too much? You might end up with Crispy Fried Brains."

Gladys Folkers and Jeanne Engelmann

You might be curious about what it's like to use an illegal drug or get drunk. (Or maybe you already know.) In a recent survey of 1,000 students ages 13–17, drugs were identified as the #1 worst influence facing today's youth. Peer pressure was #2. Drugs and peer pressure can be a deadly combination. If you want to know more about how drugs and alcohol can affect you, talk to your school counselor or school social worker. Ask for advice on resisting pressure to experiment.

 **TODAY**

I won't give in to negative peer pressure.

"I wanted to be somebody. All of us want
to be somebody. I remember so well that first
night I was able to say: 'I am a cartoonist.'"

Charles Schulz

Can you recall a time when you told yourself "YES! I
did it!" Wasn't that a great feeling? When you succeed at
something—anything—take a few moments to enjoy
the rush of positive feelings that follows. Give yourself a
pat on the back for completing a task, reaching a goal,
or being the person you want to be.

 **TODAY**

**I'll congratulate myself
on a job well done.**

"You've got to make the most
of where you are."

Anthony Edwards

Where are you right now? In your room? At school? In the bathroom? (Why not? Lots of people read in the bathroom.) Now that you know where you are in the world, go farther: Consider what's around you. Are you making the most of the resources, people, and opportunities available to you? When did you last visit your local library? Go to a museum, concert, or play? Spend time with your parents or a mentor? Visit with a teacher before or after school? Ask a caring adult for help with a problem? What else?

TODAY

**I'll take advantage of a resource
that's available to me.**

> "Don't look at your feet to see if
> you are doing it right. Just dance."
>
> *Anne Lamott*

Feeling self-conscious is a normal (if uncomfortable) part of being a teen. You might constantly wonder *Do I look okay? Am I a loser? Does everyone hate me? Am I doing this all wrong?* If you have these kinds of thoughts too often or regularly, it's hard to have fun and get things done. Try putting aside your self-doubt. Don't let it take over your life.

 **TODAY**

I won't let self-doubt ruin my day.

"Hold fast to dreams
For if dreams die,
Life is a broken-winged bird
That cannot fly."

Langston Hughes

Whatever your dreams are, don't let go. Don't let anyone talk you out of them; don't listen when they say your dreams are foolish, impossible, or wrong. As a young black American in the early part of the 20th century, Langston Hughes dreamed of being a writer; he worked on a freighter, had odd jobs, and was a busboy in a Washington, D.C., hotel when he met Vachel Lindsay, a famous poet who promoted the younger man's work. Today Hughes is remembered as one of the greatest and most influential poets of our century.

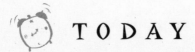 **TODAY**

I'll hold on to a dream.

"Whenever you are asked if you
can do a job, tell 'em 'certainly I can!'—
and get busy and find out how to do it."

Theodore Roosevelt

Teddy Roosevelt was willing to try almost anything
once, even if he hadn't done it before and wasn't sure
how it was done. He was the first U.S. president to
ride in a car, explore the sea in a submarine, and
soar through the skies in an airplane. He was curious,
courageous—and he had faith in himself. (P.S. Today is
Theodore Roosevelt's birthday.)

 **TODAY**

I'll have faith in myself.

"In high school, I was short and pudgy,
and I was this meek, scared guy.
But I refused to let it get to me."

David Schwimmer

Every so often, popular magazines feature old high school photos of models, movie stars, athletes, and other famous people. Usually, these celebrities look a lot better now than they did back then. Maybe they were late bloomers, or maybe they were going through an awkward stage—it doesn't really matter. What matters is they achieved their goals anyway. You can, too.

 **TODAY**

**I'll focus on my goals,
not on my appearance.**

❨OCTOBER 29❩

> "Perfectionism is self-abuse
> of the highest order."
>
> *Anne Wilson Schaef*

Are you trying to live up to the impossible standard of perfection? Then you're being too hard on yourself. Perfection doesn't exist; nobody's perfect, so why should you be? Give yourself a break—make mistakes, relax, enjoy life a little more. You'll feel better if you cut yourself some slack.

 **TODAY**

I'll ease up on myself.

> "Everyone's day has the same number of hours. If you want to do something special like writing a story, you must make time just for that."
>
> *Marion Dane Bauer*

Some people just seem to get more done. They juggle many activities—sports, homework, clubs, lessons— and still have time for volunteer work, a part-time job, and fun. What's their secret? Good time-management skills. They plan their weeks in advance and build in time for things they want to do. If you'd like to do the same, here's how: Start by filling in your daily planner or calendar with the dates and times of your regularly scheduled activities. Now see where you have free time left over. Are your Saturday mornings open? What about Tuesdays after school?

 **TODAY**

I'll schedule time for something special.

> "Optimism is the faith that leads to achievement. Nothing can be done without hope and confidence."

Helen Keller

What is hope? Emily Dickinson described it as "the thing with feathers/that perches on the soul/and sings the tune without the words/and never stops—at all." Hope lifts us, carries us along, and helps us reach for the stars. Without it, we have nothing to keep us moving forward—and nothing to look forward to.

 **TODAY**

I'll be hopeful.

✷ NOVEMBER 1 ✷

"I will remember you. Will you remember me?
Don't let your life pass you by.
Weep not for the memories."

Sarah McLachlan

We all have treasured memories of special people and times we never want to forget. You can store yours in a Memory Book that you create yourself. Use a blank book or journal to write down important events, significant moments, and funny things that happened. Describe everything in vivid detail—the sounds, tastes, smells, conversations, and so on. Add photos and other memorabilia, if you'd like. (*Tip:* This is a great thing to do with an elderly relative who will gladly reminisce with you. You may discover surprising things about your family's past.)

 TODAY

I'll start a Memory Book.

"I start with the idea that nothing
is impossible and everything
can be done in the end."

Alberta Ferretti

When it comes to success—at school, at work, in relationships, in life—attitude matters. You're more willing to take positive risks when you're optimistic about the outcome. You're more likely to use your creativity and problem-solving skills, less likely to give up before you start. Some things *are* impossible; some things *can't* be done. But you won't know unless you try…and you won't try if you're sure you'll fail.

TODAY

I'll have a positive attitude.

"It is not only for what we do
that we are held responsible,
but also for what we do not do."

Molière

After school, you notice a group of Asian students picking on a black student. The Asians are calling the black kid ugly names. You're friends with the Asian students, and you know the black student from history class. It's not your fight, and you're running late, so you ignore the scene and walk away. Question: Are you responsible? No…and yes. You're not responsible for what the Asian students say, or how the black student feels. But what about moral responsibility? Ethical responsibility? Responsibility to your friends—on both sides? Is walking away the best thing to do?

TODAY

I'll hold myself responsible.

"The only person you should ever compete with is yourself. You can't hope to find a fairer match."

Todd Ruthman

Do you often compete with other people—your friends, siblings, classmates, teammates, and the kids in your neighborhood? That's a lot of pressure to put on yourself. When you're constantly competing with or comparing yourself to others, it's hard to measure up. Instead of trying to outdo everyone else, focus on your own goals.

 **TODAY**

I'll compete with myself.

~ NOVEMBER 5 ~

"It may be a sign of character,
not of weakness, to know when
you have to ask for help."

Martha Manning

During your darkest times—or even when you're
bothered by a minor problem—there may be many
people in your life who are ready and willing to help
you. Often all you have to do is ask. Can you talk to your
parents? A teacher? A youth group leader? A religious
leader? A mentor? A neighbor? A friend? Make a list of
names and phone numbers and keep it in a safe place—
your journal, daily planner, notebook, or desk drawer.

 **TODAY**

I'll think of five people I can
ask for help when I need it.

❧ NOVEMBER 6 ❧

"Failure is the opportunity to
begin again more intelligently."

Henry Ford

History is full of successful failures—men and
women who tried, flopped, tried again, stumbled, and
ultimately got it right. Walt Disney was fired by a newspaper editor because he had "no good ideas" and he
"doodled too much." Winston Churchill flunked sixth
grade and finished last in his class when he graduated
from college; he later became England's prime minister.
Dr. Robert Jarvick was turned down by 15 American
medical schools; he later invented an artificial heart.
Diana Nyad was kicked out of college; she went on to be
a champion swimmer.

 **TODAY**

I'll see a failure as an opportunity.

"Imagination will often carry us to
worlds that never were. But without it,
we go nowhere."

Carl Sagan

What has no motor, wheels, or wings but has the power to take you anywhere you want to go? Your imagination. (Norman Vincent Peale described imagination as "the true magic carpet.") When you imagine, you use your mind to see what could be, what might be, and even what can be. Give yourself the time and space to let your imagination roam.

 **TODAY**

I'll use my imagination.

❦ NOVEMBER 8 ❦

"I'm not into working out.
My philosophy: No pain, no pain."

Carol Leifer

Do you have a similar philosophy? Is your idea of exercise getting off the couch to search for the remote control? You can improve your attitude about exercise by thinking about all the positive benefits of physical activity. First, you'll strengthen your heart, lungs, bones, and muscles. You'll also have more energy to tackle the day's challenges, and you'll sleep more soundly at night. Best of all, you'll feel stronger and more positive. (*Tip:* Exercising during your teens will help you grow into a healthier adult.)

 **TODAY**

I'll get serious about exercise.

NOVEMBER 9

"The first thing is to love your sport.
Never do it to please someone else.
It has to be yours."

Peggy Fleming

Teens who are involved in sports feel more fit and confident. Are you part of a team? Athletics can teach you about goal setting, teamwork, winning and losing, and handling pressure. If you're on a team, do you enjoy your sport? To find out if your particular sport is right for you, ask yourself these questions: *Am I having fun? Does it make me feel good? Am I inspired? Do I look forward to it?* If you can't answer yes to all four, you might want to try another activity or talk to your coach. And if you're not on a team, consider joining one.

TODAY

I'll think about a sport I'd like to play.

"My motto was always to keep swinging.
Whether I was in a slump or feeling badly
or having trouble off the field, the only
thing to do was keep swinging."

Hank Aaron

Anyone can get into a slump on or off the field. Maybe you're not on top of your game right now or you're bored with your fitness routine. One way to stay motivated is to keep a Fitness Journal. This is a place to write down anything you want about your sport, physical activities, or fitness plan. Keep a record of the goals you score or your goals for staying in shape. Write about your successes, setbacks, or slumps. Include ideas for relieving stress and staying inspired. If you want, add encouraging quotes by famous athletes.

 **TODAY**

I'll start a Fitness Journal.

"You can be pleased with nothing
when you are not pleased with yourself."

Lady Mary Wortley Montagu

Sometimes we focus more on the negative side of
our personality than the positive side. You can make a
conscious effort to focus on the good side.

- Instead of thinking "I'm too emotional," try
  thinking "I show my feelings."
- Instead of "I'm too shy," try "I'm reserved."
- Instead of "I'm pushy," try "I'm assertive."
- Instead of "I'm nosy," try "I'm curious."
- Instead of "I'm weird," try "I'm creative."
- Instead of "I'm too ____," try "I'm ____."

(Which personality trait would you like to feel
better about?)

 **TODAY**

I'm pleased with myself.

❧ NOVEMBER 12 ❧

> "Within your heart, keep one still,
> secret spot where dreams may go."

Louise Driscoll

Imagine your country is at war, and you and your family must seek shelter from the enemy. You leave everything behind to secretly hide in an attic room, desperately hoping to survive. This happened to Anne Frank, a 13-year-old Jewish girl in Amsterdam during World War II. For two years, she hid from the Nazis, unable to go outdoors, breathe fresh air, or feel the sun on her face. One thing that sustained her was her dreams. She once confided to her diary: "My greatest wish is to be a journalist, and later on, a great writer." Her famous diary is one of the best-loved books of all time.

 **TODAY**

I'll hold onto a dream.

"When I was diagnosed at age twelve
with a chronic illness, I felt as if a door had
shut right in my face. It took me a long time
to see that another door was opening for me."

Kelly Huegel

Learning you have a medical problem can be one of the scariest things you'll ever face. Whether you're sick or have to spend time in the hospital, fear, dread, even panic might be your first reaction. Kelly Huegel learned to deal with her fear, and she wrote a book about her experience. She says that the #1 way to cope is to face your fears. Start by getting information about your medical condition and any procedures you might undergo. Ask questions. Do your research. Understand what's ahead of you. Once you know what you're up against, you can face it with courage.

 **TODAY**

I'll face a fear.

"I am forthright, I suppose,
but what else should one be?"

Jamaica Kincaid

To be forthright means to be honest, direct, and genuine. What else should you be? Dishonest? Insincere? A fake? Reflect on how you've acted during the past few days or weeks—how you've related to the people in your life (and to yourself). Would you describe yourself as a forthright person? If not, why not? Often it's hard to be honest; we worry about getting in trouble, losing face, or hurting other people. And sometimes it's hard to face the truth about ourselves. (*Tip:* It gets easier with practice.)

 **TODAY**

I'll be forthright.

⌁ NOVEMBER 15 ⌁

> "When nobody around you seems
> to measure up, it's time to
> check your yardstick."
>
> *Bill Lemley*

Do you have perfectionist parents? When you bring home your report card, does your dad notice the lowest grade first? After your basketball game, does your mom point out the shots you missed instead of congratulating you on the ones you made? Perfectionist parents expect you to aim for their impossible standards; they demand 110 percent all the time. You might end up feeling like a failure. If your parents treat you this way, tell them how much it hurts. Explain that you're trying your best and you need their support. It may be uncomfortable to talk about it, but you'll feel better afterwards.

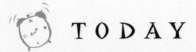 **TODAY**

**I'll think about whether
my parents are perfectionists.**

❧ NOVEMBER 16 ❧

> "Take calculated risks. That is quite
> different from being rash."

George S. Patton

When you're considering taking a risk, ask yourself these questions:

1. What are the risks involved?
2. What have I got to gain?
3. What have I got to lose?
4. Do the things I might gain justify the things I might lose? Do the positives outweigh the negatives?
5. What are my chances of succeeding?

If there's time—if you don't need to decide quickly whether to take the risk—talk it over with someone you trust. Get his or her perspective.

TODAY

I'll take a calculated risk.

⚘ NOVEMBER 17 ⚘

"When people love each other, they share
what's going on in their lives. It's okay
to be honest, even if that honesty proves
you're in trouble or made a mistake."

Richard Carlson

Sometimes it's hard to admit a mistake or failure, even
(or especially) to people we love. But it helps. Talk about
what's going on in your life, what's bothering you, what
you need. Let people in. They want to help.

 TODAY

I'll talk to a loved one.

NOVEMBER 18

"I never think about why something
hasn't been done already; I think about
why nobody has done it right yet."

Marcia Kilgore

There were already plenty of day spas in New York City
when Marcia Kilgore decided to start one. She didn't let
the competition stop her or scare her. Instead, she
opened her Bliss Spa in SoHo—and by 1998, she was
booking more than 40,000 appointments a year for
people craving her famous facials, body polishes, and
manicures. Entrepreneurs trust their instincts and
believe they can succeed. They love what they do, and
they stay focused on their goals no matter what.

TODAY

I'll think like an entrepreneur.

"Standing up for myself and deciding
to be my own person was the smartest
thing I did growing up."

Jennifer Love Hewitt

Do you sometimes feel like you're ruled by your parents, teachers, friends, classmates, or the world in general? Does it seem like your thoughts, opinions, and wishes don't count? Speak up and let people know what you're thinking. Express your feelings and don't be afraid to say "This is what I think" or "Here's how I feel" or "I'd like to try it this way instead." People who care about you will listen—and they'll respect you more.

 **TODAY**

I'll stand up for myself.

~ NOVEMBER 20 ~

"Life is what happens while you are
making other plans."

John Lennon

Some people are super-planners. They make daily
plans (do homework, work out), weekly plans (finish
science project, volunteer), monthly plans (go to a concert, join a youth group), yearly plans (find a summer
job), five-year plans (get into college), ten-year plans
(have a good job, get married), even twenty-year plans
(climb Mt. Everest). Planning is great—as long as you
don't let your plans control you. A good plan is a guide,
not a dictator. It changes as circumstances change, and
as you change.

 **TODAY**

I won't let my plans control me.

❧ NOVEMBER 21 ❧

"The best way to escape from
a problem is to solve it."

Alan Saporta

There are many reasons not to solve a problem. Problem solving takes time and effort (sometimes a *lot* of time and effort). It can be scary—especially when the problem involves another person, and we're not sure how he or she will react to our efforts. Plus it's easier to procrastinate, make excuses, even ignore the problem entirely. But most problems don't just go away. And sometimes they get bigger and uglier.

 **TODAY**

I'll tackle a problem I've been avoiding.

❧ NOVEMBER 22 ❧

"Dreams have as much influence as actions."

Stéphane Mallarmé

You're staring out the window at a butterfly, watching it dart from flower to flower, and soon you're floating away, drifting, imagining yourself in a far-off place…in a hang glider, diving off a high cliff, sailing through the air, the wind in your face and blue sky all around you. What's going on? You're in a daydream, where anything is possible and anything can happen. Your imagination has taken over. Let yourself daydream now. Relax. Breathe deeply. See the sights, listen to the sounds, smell the smells. Take a trip in your mind.

 **TODAY**

I'll daydream.

> "One loses many laughs
> by not laughing at oneself."

Sara Jeannette Duncan

Everyone does dumb, silly, embarrassing things—including you. But what do you do next? Slink off and go into hiding? Scold yourself for being an idiot? Strike out at anyone who dares to laugh at you? Being able to laugh at yourself is a valuable skill. It relieves tension and puts other people at ease. It takes power away from those who make fun of misfortunes; their laughter can't hurt you if you're already laughing at yourself. Plus it feels good to laugh, and you should do it whenever you can!

TODAY

I'll laugh at myself.

"A joy that is shared is a joy made double."

English proverb

Maya was thrilled to learn she was a finalist in the senior writing contest. She was just about to tell her best friend Dierdre when she stopped herself: What if Dierdre was jealous? Or didn't think it was a big deal? Or worse, what if sharing the news was bad luck and ruined Maya's chances of winning the contest? Maya decided it was silly to think this way, and she told Dierdre about being a finalist. Dierdre gave her a hug and said "Whether you win or not, I couldn't be more proud of you." Maya felt great for the rest of the day.

 **TODAY**

**I'll share my good fortune
or delight in someone else's.**

> "Life is short, and when you want
> something, you really do have to go for it."
>
> *Kate Winslet*

What do you want right now, this minute? To be captain of the soccer team? An A on your biology test? The lead in the school play? More friends? A summer job? Whatever your goal may be, take the first step toward reaching it. After you've taken the first step, you'll have the confidence to take the next step…and the next.

 **TODAY**

I'll go for it.

∾ NOVEMBER 26 ∾

"Nothing in this world can take
the place of persistence."

Calvin Coolidge

The 30th president of the United States, Calvin Coolidge was known for being reserved and cautious—but once he grabbed onto a problem, he didn't let it go until he solved it. He went on to say: "Talent will not [take the place of persistence]; nothing is more common than unsuccessful people with talent. Genius will not; unrewarded genius is almost a proverb. Education will not; the world is full of educated derelicts. Persistence and determination alone are omnipotent. The slogan 'press on' has solved and always will solve the problems of the human race."

 **TODAY**

I'll be persistent.

NOVEMBER 27

"The only certainty is that nothing is certain."

Pliny the Elder

The first answer to a problem isn't always the right answer. *Example:* If you have a problem with a student of another race, don't immediately assume it's a racial conflict. Some problems that are quickly labeled "racially motivated" are really *people problems*—difficulties getting along, seeing eye-to-eye, communicating, and/or respecting each other that any two people might experience, regardless of their race.

 **TODAY**

I won't jump to conclusions.

"The chains of habit are too weak to be felt until they are too strong to be broken."

Samuel Johnson

"One little drink can't hurt." "I'll smoke this last cigarette, then I'll quit." "This drug won't hurt me if I only try it once." Have you told yourself these little lies? Nobody means to develop a bad habit. Bad habits sneak up on us, and once they're formed, they're hard to break. You can decide *now* to resist behaviors that might become harmful habits—such as smoking or using alcohol and other drugs. Be confident in your decision not to experiment, practice saying no, and don't worry that other people might think you're wimpy or boring. In fact, you're proving the opposite.

 **TODAY**

I'll say no way.

"Whenever you find yourself on the side of
the majority, it is time to pause and reflect."

Mark Twain

It's easy and comfortable to go along with the crowd.
That way, you fit in and don't make waves. But is the
majority always right? You might want to do some
research into this question, or talk it over with a history
teacher. Or reflect on your own experiences—times
when you've thought, believed, or acted a certain way
because "everybody else" was doing it. (In the fairy tale
"The Emperor's New Clothes," a child is the only one
brave enough to say that the emperor is really naked.)

 **TODAY**

I won't just go along with the crowd.

"There cannot be mental atrophy in any person
who continues to observe, to remember
what he observes, and to seek answers for his
unceasing hows and whys about things."

Alexander Graham Bell

During his 75 years, Alexander Graham Bell invented the telephone, started the Bell Telephone Company, founded the journal *Science,* served as president of the National Geographic Society, and much more. He knew all about preventing "mental atrophy"—also known as brain rot. Scientists who study the brain have found that when you learn something new, this creates more links between your brain cells. It's amazingly easy to learn something new. Pay attention in class, read an article or a book, check out a Web site, or ask a question. Be a curious cat.

TODAY

I'll learn something new.

❖ DECEMBER 1 ❖

"You must never be fearful about
what you are doing when it is right."

Rosa Parks

On December 1, 1955, in the segregated South of the
United States, Rosa Parks was riding the bus after a long
day's work. She was tired, and when a white man asked
her to give up her seat, she refused to move. The law at
the time said that only white people could sit at the
front of the bus, so she was arrested. Her action began
the Civil Rights movement of the 1950s and made her
an enduring symbol of strength and courage. Rosa
Parks took a stand…by staying seated.

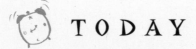 **TODAY**

I'll take a stand.

◈ DECEMBER 2 ◈

"As you ramble on through life, brother,
whatever be your goal: Keep your eyes
upon the donut and not upon the hole!"

Murray Banks

This silly rhyme is worth memorizing. It's short, easy, and good advice besides. As you're working toward your goals, stay positive. Focus on winning. Assume that you'll get there. Never underestimate the power of positive thinking. The great athletes know this: They envision themselves hitting the ball, kicking the goal, making the basket, crossing the finishing line, or completing the triple toe loop.

 **TODAY**

I'll see the donut, not the hole.

❖ DECEMBER 3 ❖

"To dream of the person you would like
to be is to waste the person you are."

Anonymous

Do you sometimes (or often) wish you could leave
your life behind and be somebody else? A celebrity,
sports figure, model, politician, movie star, or…? Most
people fantasize about being someone famous—often
someone who's rich, successful, and has a "perfect"
body. It's fun but frustrating for obvious reasons; there's
just no way you can become that person. All you can
become is yourself.

 **TODAY**

I'll dream of the person I am.

◈ DECEMBER 4 ◈

"You can get through life with bad manners,
but it's easier with good manners."

Lillian Gish

You're too tired to do laundry so you head off to school in a dirty shirt. You barge onto the bus so you can get a good seat. You let out a huge burp during lunch to amuse your friends. To entertain yourself during geography, you pick on a boy sitting in front of you, call him a dork, and flick him on the head. How rude! Do manners matter? Yes! Having manners and being polite is a way of showing you have respect not only for others, but also for yourself.

 **TODAY**

I'll be polite.

❖ DECEMBER 5 ❖

"Lying is done with words
and also with silence."

Adrienne Rich

Zach was a taking a test in history class when he noticed Angie copying answers from another student. Cheating was forbidden, and according to school policy, students who witnessed cheating were supposed to tell a teacher. Zach wasn't sure if he should report Angie. She was pretty and popular, and he didn't want to get on her bad side. After thinking it over, he decided that Angie really wasn't hurting anyone by cheating, and he didn't report her. Did he do the right thing?

 **TODAY**

I'll be truthful.

◈ DECEMBER 6 ◈

"You can run with the big dogs
or sit on the porch and bark."

Wallace Arnold

In a recent Public Agenda survey of 1,300 high school students, half said that drugs and violence were serious problems in their schools. If you don't feel safe at school—because of drugs, violence, bullying, discrimination, harassment, or any reason—you have a choice. You can complain...or you can take action. Form a committee of other students who feel the way you do. Find an adult sponsor—a teacher, coach, or school counselor—who's willing to work with you. Then brainstorm solutions and choose one or more to try.

 **TODAY**

**I'll stop complaining about a problem
and do something about it.**

"I am not afraid of storms,
for I am learning how to sail my ship."

Louisa May Alcott

Everyone fears something (and some people fear almost everything). Psychologists believe that our fears can influence and even control our behavior, and that overcoming our fears can make us stronger and more capable. What scares you? Are you afraid of the unknown (ghosts, monsters, aliens)? Of people you know (your parents, teachers, doctors)? Do you fear flying in an airplane, speaking in front of a group, standing on the highest floor of a skyscraper, or sleeping in a totally dark room? Naming your fears—and admitting them—is the first step toward tackling them.

 **TODAY**

I'll work to overcome a fear.

❖ DECEMBER 8 ❖

"I've learned that when something
seems like the worst thing,
it may be the best thing."

Lea Thompson

There's an old story about a man who had 20 stallions.
One day, they all ran away into the hills. The man
cursed his bad luck—until the 20 stallions reappeared
with 20 mares. Later, when his son fell from one of the
mares and broke his leg, the man was disappointed and
cried "This is very bad!" Then a battalion of soldiers
stormed through the village, collecting all the young
men for battle—except for the son, who couldn't fight
with a broken leg. The man said "Perhaps, in this case, a
broken leg is good."

TODAY

**I'll look for the gift inside
the disappointment.**

"Prosperity is a way of living and thinking, and not just money or things. Poverty is a way of living and thinking, and not just a lack of money or things."

Eric Butterworth

You can have a ton of stuff and still feel empty inside. If you're not doing anything meaningful with your life—if you don't have goals to work toward, if you're not learning and growing and reaching out—all the material things in the world won't matter. On the other hand, it doesn't take money or possessions to touch someone else's life with kindness or service. And the satisfaction that comes from that can make you feel like the world's richest person.

 **TODAY**

I'll decide if I'm prosperous or poor.

❖ DECEMBER 10 ❖

"Without faith, nothing is possible.
With it, nothing is impossible."

Mary McLeod Bethune

According to a 1998 poll of over 1,000 Americans, faith matters. *USA Weekend* reported that "next to individual and family health, faith is most important to being happy." Many young people drop out of their congregations during their teens. Organized religion no longer seems relevant to their lives. If you're involved with a faith community, don't drop out until you talk it over with your youth leader or spiritual leader. If you're not involved with a faith community and you think you'd like to be, visit congregations in your neighborhood or nearby. Talk with the people who lead the youth program.

 **TODAY**

**I'll believe in something
bigger than myself.**

"A man wrapped up in himself
makes a very small bundle."

Benjamin Franklin

Ten-year-old Megan Leaf wanted to help kids at the Johns Hopkins Children's Center, where she had been a patient herself. So she began filling hand-decorated bags with toys, coloring books, and other items to calm children undergoing treatment in the pediatric emergency room. What began as an act of kindness turned into a nonprofit business—Love Box, Limited—which now serves thousands of sick children. Megan wasn't motivated by personal gain, but helping others has brought her some wonderful rewards: the smiles from all the sick kids she's helped, and a feeling that her actions have made a positive difference in the world.

 **TODAY**

I'll give the gift of my time or service.

"It's easy to forget your troubles
when you're on the dance floor."

Sandra Bullock

Sandra Bullock goes salsa dancing after a hard day. Liv
Tyler turns the music up loud whenever she's feeling
down. Other celebrities say that working out, watching
movies, or hanging around with friends can take their
minds off their troubles. What works for you? Do you
feel better when you talk to people? (Then give someone a call.) Does your mood improve when you get
some exercise? (Dance, work out, or go swimming.) Do
you need quiet time alone? (Write in your journal or
take a walk.)

 **TODAY**

**I'll do something that
always makes me feel better.**

❖ DECEMBER 13 ❖

"Stress is an ignorant state. It believes
that everything is an emergency."

Natalie Goldberg

Are the holidays stressful for you? They are for many
people. For some reason, a time of year that's supposed
to be joyful is anything but. Maybe we expect too much
of ourselves and each other. Maybe we squeeze in too
many things—parties, obligations, decorations, shop-
ping, wrapping, entertaining—and don't leave enough
time for relaxation and reflection. If your family
holidays are filled with fights and arguments, you can
try to break that tradition. Have a family meeting to talk
about ways to make the holidays pleasant and meaningful for everyone.

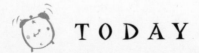

TODAY

**I'll think ahead to the holidays—and
how they might be happier at home.**

"You can't cure stress by thinking
about it or worrying about it."

Earl Hipp

Here are five ways to lessen stress during the holidays
and all year long:

1. Think back to other times when you've coped
   with a tough time, situation, or event. Recycle
   strategies that worked.

2. Find someone to talk to—someone who
   will listen and, if you want, offer honest,
   respectful advice.

3. If you don't know how to relax, learn how. You
   might try the exercises on pages 78, 79, and 117.

4. Laugh. Laughter is a proven stress reducer.

5. Simplify. Make a list of things you *must* do,
   then cross out at least five.

TODAY

I'll practice ways to lessen stress.

◈ DECEMBER 15 ◈

"Practice random acts of kindness
and senseless beauty."

Bumper sticker

Any act of kindness, however small, benefits at least
two people: the person you were kind to *and* you.
So leave a note in your mom's briefcase, pick up litter
from the sidewalk in front of your house, buy lunch for
your best friend, make a charitable donation, visit with
an elderly neighbor, or whatever you'd like to do.
The possibilities are endless. As author James Barrie
(*Peter Pan*) once said, "Those who bring sunshine to
the lives of others cannot keep it from themselves."
Tip: This is another great way to lessen stress.

 **TODAY**

I'll do a random act of kindness.

"I seem to have an awful lot
of people inside me."

Dame Edith Evans

Cameron is polite to his teachers but rude to his parents. Elly pretends to be dumb in math because she wants Max to like her. Sam has a dream he's never shared with anyone: More than anything, he wants to be a dancer someday. Silas pretends to be tough—in his actions, the way he dresses, the way he talks—but deep down, he's a gentle person. Moira goes along with the crowd, even when she doesn't agree with them. Which of the people inside you is the real you?

TODAY

I'll be the real me.

"No problem is so big
that you can't run away from it."

Snoopy

Make a list of the problems you're facing in your life.
Major ones, minor ones, new ones, old ones…write
them all down. Now analyze your list. Which problems
are you actively trying to solve? Which ones have you
been running away from? Pick *one* problem from
the latter category. Do something about it—starting
today. *Tip:* See the Creative Problem Solving steps and
suggestions on pages 278 and 279.

TODAY

**I'll face a problem
I've been running away from.**

"Could we change our attitude,
we should not only see life differently,
but life itself would come to be different."

Katherine Mansfield

Author and popular speaker Cassandra Walker was extremely self-conscious about her appearance when she was growing up. Other kids called her names like "Big Lips" and "African Jungle Mouth." She felt so bad about the teasing that she would hold in her lips by biting her bottom lip with her teeth. One day, her mom remarked that full lips were part of the African American heritage, and Cassandra suddenly saw things in a different light. She realized her mother had full lips, too, and her mother was beautiful. Cassandra stopped worrying about what other kids said. As her self-confidence increased, the teasing *decreased*.

TODAY

I'll feel good about myself.

"Arriving at the goal is
the starting point to another."

John Dewey

You did it—you received the award, won the election, made the team, or got the job. You accomplished what you set out to do, earned high fives from all your friends, and, for a while, felt great. But now you feel a little empty and let down. It's normal to have a sense of "What now?" after reaching a goal. Instead of thinking of it as the *end* of something, consider it the *beginning*. Now you can pursue an even higher goal or a bigger dream. What are you waiting for?

 **TODAY**

I'll plan my next goal.

❖ DECEMBER 20 ❖

"To make the world a friendly place,
one must show it a friendly face."

James Whitcomb Riley

If you want to make more friends, be friendly. Wear a smile, look cheerful, and learn to make people laugh. Introduce yourself, invite people to join you, and practice your conversation skills. Even if you're naturally shy, get involved in more activities at school and in your community so you'll have a chance to meet more people. William E. Holler said, "One thing everybody in the world wants and needs is a little friendliness."

 **TODAY**

I'll be friendly.

"To be the best at some things,
you have to give up other things."

Se Ri Pak

As a 20-year-old rookie, South Korean-born Se Ri Pak won four important golf tournaments in 10 weeks. She decided at age 14 to focus only on golf, and her efforts paid off—but not without a price. "Sometimes I wish I could just be like other 20-year-olds," she told an interviewer. "Just have a normal life." Is there something you want to be best at? Are you willing to make the sacrifices? Or is it more important to keep a balance in your life?

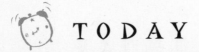 **TODAY**

**I'll think about whether my dreams
are doable—and worth what I'll have
to give up to reach them.**

◈ DECEMBER 22 ◈

> "You cannot make progress
> without making decisions."
>
> *Jim Rohn*

Some decisions are easy ("Tacos or lasagna?" "The blue shirt or the red one?") and some are tough ("Should I make friends with that person?" "Should I admit a mistake?"). Your days and weeks are full of decisions, and there's no way to avoid them. Even *not* deciding is a type of decision, since you're choosing to let other people or circumstances decide for you. You might spend part of today taking stock of recent decisions you've made—or haven't made. Are you making progress or standing still?

 **TODAY**

I'll decide.

❖ DECEMBER 23 ❖

"Like what you do in life, do it the best
you can every day, and be honest about it."

Pat Buckley Moss

Here's the secret to living well: *Liking who you are and what you do.* Life becomes more interesting, exciting, and challenging when you feel good about yourself and what you're trying to accomplish. If you *don't* like yourself, think about why. Do you feel bad about your appearance? Are other people teasing you? Is your family having problems? Identifying the reasons behind your low self-esteem is the first step toward changing your situation for the better.

 **TODAY**

I like who I am.

◈ DECEMBER 24 ◈

"You can complain because roses have thorns,
or you can rejoice because thorns have roses."

Ziggy

It all depends on your attitude. Your glass can be half empty or half full, the sky partly cloudy or partly sunny, an apple shiny and delicious or flawed by a single spot. Viktor Frankl spent three years in the Nazi concentration camps at Auschwitz during World War II. He could easily have lost all hope, but he didn't. He remained optimistic about his future. In *Man's Search for Meaning*, he wrote: "Everything can be taken from a man but one thing: the last of human freedoms—to choose one's own attitude in any given set of circumstances."

 **TODAY**

I'll rejoice.

❖ DECEMBER 25 ❖

"There is nothing stronger
in the world than gentleness."

Han Suyin

A steady drip of water turns a rock into a pebble. The flow of a river carves the Grand Canyon. A kind word lifts someone's spirits to the skies. Gentleness, mercy, tenderness—these are powerful forces in the world and in our relationships. If you don't know your own strength, try being gentle.

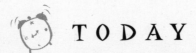 **TODAY**

I'll be gentle.

◈ DECEMBER 26 ◈

> "I will permit no man to narrow and degrade my soul by making me hate him."
>
> *Booker T. Washington*

Hatred is a poisonous emotion. It eats away at your dreams, goals, hopes, and ambitions like acid. It can become all-consuming. When you're full of hatred, you're so angry and bitter that you can't possibly feel good about yourself. Even if someone provokes you, injures you, persecutes you, or just plain disgusts you, don't let hatred sneak into your heart and soul. Resist it. Fight it. Talk with someone you trust (a parent, teacher, religious leader, or other wise person); get his or her perspective and advice.

 **TODAY**

I refuse to hate.

❖ DECEMBER 27 ❖

"I'm five-feet-four, but I always feel six-foot-one, tall and strong."

Yvette Mimieux

Because actress Yvette Mimieux *tells* herself she's tall and strong, that's how she *feels*. Your self-talk has a profound and lasting effect on your self-esteem. When you make a mistake, do you think *Everyone makes mistakes* or *I'm so stupid?* When you succeed at something, do you think *I did it!* or *I was lucky?* Whenever you have a negative thought about yourself—when your self-talk makes you feel bad—change it to a positive thought. Do this immediately. You'll feel better and you'll form the habit of self-affirmation, which most successful people share.

 **TODAY**

I'll watch my self-talk.

◈ DECEMBER 28 ◈

"Self-esteem comes from within."

Drew Barrymore

What does it mean to have high self-esteem? Does it mean you think you're better than everyone else? Or that you've convinced yourself that you're smarter, stronger, funnier, wiser, or whatever than you really are? That's not it at all. Self-esteem isn't about inflating your own self-image. It's about respecting yourself and taking pride in who you are. How do you feel about yourself right now?

 **TODAY**

I'll check my self-esteem.

◈ DECEMBER 29 ◈

"Try a thing you haven't done three times.
Once, to get over the fear of doing it. Twice,
to learn how to do it. And a third time,
to figure out whether you like it or not."

Virgil Thomson

Life is full of potential new experiences and positive
risks. Give them a try. Let curiosity motivate you; don't
let fear stop you. Then decide for yourself if you should
make them a regular part of who you are.

 TODAY

I'll be open to new experiences.

❖ DECEMBER 30 ❖

"It is good to have an end to journey toward;
but it is the journey that matters, in the end."

Ursula K. Le Guin

This year is nearly over and a new year is about to begin. As you think about where you want to go—the goals you want to reach for, the problems you want to solve, how you want to feel about yourself in the months ahead—you might start by reviewing where you've been. If you've kept a journal, this is the perfect day to read through it. How have you changed? How have you grown? What have you learned? What insights can you gain from the experiences you've had and the choices you've made?

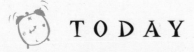 **T O D A Y**

I'll look back.

> "The world is round and the place
> which may seem like the end
> may also be the beginning."

Ivy Baker Priest

You've reached the last daily reading in this book, but it's not the end. In fact, this book doesn't really have an end—or a beginning. Today you're reading page 366; tomorrow, if you want, you'll read page 1. Depending on which calendar you use—Gregorian, Hebrew, Chinese, Moslem, Bahá'í, World, Julian, etc. (there are more)—it might not even be December 31. No matter what the date is, we hope you'll keep solving problems, setting goals, and feeling good about yourself.

 **TODAY**

I'll look forward.

366

Subject Index

People (and others) Index

Portions of this book include information that has been adapted or excerpted from the following Free Spirit Publishing titles, with permission of the publisher:

The Best of Free Spirit: Five Years of Award-Winning News and Views on Growing Up by The Free Spirit Editors

Dreams Can Help: A Journal Guide to Understanding Your Dreams and Making Them Work for You by Jonni Kincher

The Families Book: True Stories About Real Kids and the People They Live With and Love by Arlene Erlbach

The Gifted Kids' Survival Guide: A Teen Handbook by Judy Galbraith, M.A., and Jim Delisle, Ph.D.

How Rude! The Teenagers' Guide to Good Manners, Proper Behavior, and Not Grossing People Out by Alex J. Packer, Ph.D.

The Right Moves: A Girl's Guide to Getting Fit and Feeling Good by Tina Schwager, P.T.A., A.T.,C., and Michele Schuerger

Stories from My Life: Cassandra Walker Talks to Teens About Growing Up by Cassandra Walker

Succeeding with LD (Learning Differences): 20 True Stories About People with LD by Jill Lauren, M.A.

Totally Private and Personal: Journaling Ideas for Girls and Young Women by Jessica Wilber

What Kids Need to Succeed: Proven, Practical Ways to Raise Good Kids by Peter Benson, Ph.D., Judy Galbraith, M.A., and Pamela Espeland

What Teens Need to Succeed: Proven, Practical Ways to Shape Your Own Future by Peter Benson, Ph.D., Judy Galbraith, M.A., and Pamela Espeland

When Nothing Matters Anymore: A Survival Guide for Depressed Teens by Bev Cobain, R.N.,C.

About the Authors

Pamela Espeland has written and coauthored many books for teens, children, and adults including *Life Lists for Teens, What Teens Need to Succeed, What Kids Need to Succeed, Stick Up for Yourself!, Succeed Every Day, Making the Most of Today,* and *Bringing Out the Best.* She lives in Minneapolis, Minnesota, with her husband, John Whiting, their cat, Happy, and two miniature dachshunds, Lily and Chloe.

Elizabeth Verdick is a children's book writer and editor. She is the author of many books including *Teeth Are Not for Biting* board book, *Words Are Not for Hurting* paperback, *Words Are Not for Hurting* board book, and coauthor of *Stress Can Really Get on Your Nerves!* and *True or False? Tests Stink!* (with Trevor Romain) and *How to Take the GRRRR Out of Anger* (with Marjorie Lisovskis). She lives in Minnesota with her husband and their two children.

Pamela and Elizabeth also are the coauthors of the Adding Assets Series for Kids.

Other Great Books from Free Spirit

Making the Most of Today

Daily Readings for Young People on Self-Awareness, Creativity, & Self-Esteem
by Pamela Espeland and Rosemary Wallner

Quotes from famous figures guide you through a year of positive thinking, problem solving, and practical life skills—the keys to making the most of every day. For ages 11 & up.

$10.95; 392 pp.; softcover; 4¼" x 6¼"

Fighting Invisible Tigers

A Stress Management Guide for Teens
Revised & Updated
by Earl Hipp

Proven, practical advice for teens on coping with stress, taking risks, making decisions, staying healthy, dealing with fears, building relationships, and more. For ages 11 & up.

$12.95; 160 pp.; softcover; illust.; 6" x 9"

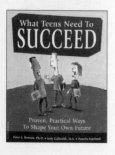

What Teens Need to Succeed

Proven, Practical Ways to Shape Your Own Future
by Peter L. Benson, Ph.D., Judy Galbraith, M.A., and Pamela Espeland

Based on a national survey, this book describes 40 Developmental Assets all teens need to succeed in life, then gives hundreds of suggestions teens can use to build assets wherever they are. For ages 11 & up.

$15.95; 368 pp.; softcover; illust.; 7¼" x 9¼"